Economics

Economics

Volume 6

Economic history

GROLIER
EDUCATIONAL

Sherman Turnpike,
Danbury, Connecticut
06816

Published 2000 by Grolier Educational
Sherman Turnpike
Danbury, Connecticut 06816

© 2000 Brown Partworks Ltd

Set ISBN: 0-7172-9492-7
Volume ISBN: 0-7172-9571-0

Library of Congress Cataloging-in-Publication Data
Economics.
     p. cm.
     Includes index.
     Contents: v. 1 Money, banking, and finance — v. 2.
Business operations — v. 3. The citizen and the
economy — v. 4. The U.S. economy and the world —
v. 5. Economic theory — v. 6. History of economics
     ISBN 0-7172-9492-7 (set: alk. paper). — ISBN 0-7172-
9482-X (v. 1: alk. paper). — ISBN 0-7172-9483-8 (v. 2:
alk. paper). — ISBN 0-7172-9484-6 (v. 3: alk. paper). —
ISBN 0-7172-9485-4 (v. 4: alk. paper). — ISBN 0-7172-
9570-2 (v. 5: alk. paper). — ISBN 0-7172-9571-0 (v. 6:
alk. paper).
     1. Economics—Juvenile literature [1. Economics.] I.
Grolier Educational Corporation.

HB183. E26 2000
330—dc21   00-020414

For information address the publisher:
Grolier Educational, Sherman Turnpike,
Danbury, Connecticut 06816

FOR BROWN PARTWORKS LTD

Project editor:
Jane Lanigan
Editors: Tim Cooke,
Julian Flanders, Mike
Janson, Henry Russell
Editorial assistance:
Wendy Horobin,
Tim Mahoney,
Sally McEachern,
Chris Wiegand
Design: Tony Cohen,
Bradley Davis,
Matthew Greenfield
Picture research:
Helen Simm

Graphics: Mark Walker
Indexer:
Kay Ollerenshaw
Project consultant:
Robert Pennington,
Associate Professor,
College of Business
Administration, University
of Central Florida
Volume consultant:
Dr. Jack Morgan,
University of Louisville
Text: James Hughes

About this book

Economics is all around us. It covers almost
every aspect of life today, from how much
money you have in your pocket to the price of
real estate, from how much tax people pay to
the causes of wars in distant lands. In today's
world it is essential to understand how to manage your money, how to save wisely, and how
to shop around for good deals. It is also important to know the bigger picture: how financial
institutions work, how wealth is created and
distributed, how economics relates to politics,
and how the global economy works that ties
together everyone on the planet.

   Economics places everyday financial
matters in the wider context of the sometimes
mysterious economic forces that shape our
lives, tracing the emergence of economic doctrines and explaining how economic systems
worked in the past and how they work now.

   Each of the six books covers a particular area of economics, from personal finance to
the world economy. Five books are split into
chapters that explore their themes in depth.
Volume 5, Economic Theory, is arranged as an A-
Z encyclopedia of shorter articles about fundamental concepts in economics and can be used
as an accessible reference when reading the
rest of the set. At the end of every chapter or
article a See Also box refers you to related articles elsewhere in the set, allowing you to further investigate topics of particular interest.

   The books contain many charts and
diagrams to explain important data clearly and
explain their significance. There are also special
boxes throughout the set that highlight particular subjects in greater detail. They might explain
how to fill out a check correctly, analyze the
theory proposed by a particular economist, or
tell a story that shows how economic theory
relates to events in our everyday lives.

   If you are not sure where to find a
subject, look it up in the set index in each
volume. The index covers all six books, so it
will help you trace topics throughout the set.
There is also a glossary at the end of the book,
which provides a brief explanation of some of
the key words and phrases that occur throughout the volumes. The extensive Further Reading
list contains many of the most recent books
about different areas of economics to allow you
to do your own research. It also features a list
of useful web sites where you can find up-to-
date information and statistics.

Contents

Economic history

Early economies

From the beginnings of civilization to the rise and fall of the great cultures of the ancient world and the emergence of medieval Europe, all economies remained primarily agricultural. Urbanization and technological developments, however, made economies increasingly complex.

The study of economics is a relatively modern phenomenon, but the concerns of economists—the creation and distribution of wealth, property, and so on—have shaped human history since the beginnings of civilization. Basic to economics is the idea of satisfying wants. Economists generally consider these wants to be unlimited, which leads to barter as simple societies try to satisfy their wants. Before the emergence of fixed governments, economic theories, or money-based societies, what we now call economics related largely to the provision of food, shelter, and fuel to support a family, household, or village. Such concerns are indicated by the etymology of the word *economics* itself. It derives from a combination of the Greek *oikos*, meaning house, and *nomos*, which means law or rule. The close association with economics with the idea of prudent housekeeping continues to be stressed by some modern governments that

liken managing a national economy to managing a household budget.

Economic ideas are essentially a way of interpreting the world, however, and so they have varied throughout history and often from place to place. During the 17th and 18th centuries in Europe, for example, the subject was generally termed "political economy," relating economic concerns more closely to the idea of national and international power, which then dominated much European thinking.

The instinct to trade

The Scottish "father of economics," Adam Smith (1723–1790), observed in his classic 1776 work *The Wealth of Nations*, which formulated neoclassical economic theory, "the propensity to truck, barter, and exchange one thing for another" is an intrinsic part of human nature. For many millennia in the evolution of human society people lived nomadic lives as

ABOVE: Achievements of the ancient world, such as the pyramids of Egypt, are evidence of economically advanced societies that could organize and support vast supplies of labor.

hunter-gatherers, moving from place to place to find fruit, game, or fish to eat. Even before the emergence of settled societies, however, different communities that came into contact exchanged goods in the form of barter. If one group had a commodity the other wanted—if, for example, it had come from a place where fish were particularly abundant—then it would exchange it for something it wanted in return. Such exchanges would have followed modern economic laws of supply and demand, meaning that the rarer something was, the more of another good it could raise in any exchange.

The first farmers

Among the first producers were farmers. "Housekeeping" economics only began to take form when humankind ceased its nomadic ways and began instead to occupy permanent settlements. This profound change came with the development of agriculture. During the Neolithic period, also called the New Stone Age, probably through a combination of observation and chance, certain groups

of people around the world learned how to plant and grow crops.

Archeologists still debate the impulse that made people start farming. Some suggest that the growing population made it more difficult to find game and plants in the wild. The change took place over a long period: it began about 10,000 years ago in the Near East, from where it spread slowly into Europe; people started farming some 8,000 years ago in China and a little later in Mesoamerica. Learning how to select the best grains, the soils that suited them best, and what time of year to plant them took many centuries. Selective breeding, however, gradually evolved domestic crops that yielded more produce than their wild ancestors. People also began stock-rearing, gradually evolving the forerunners of modern domesticated species such as pigs and turkeys.

The Neolithic Revolution

The development of farming sparked the "Neolithic revolution" as people began to form permanent settlements in cultivable

LEFT: This Egyptian tomb painting shows both agriculture and, at top right, a miscreant being punished for not paying his taxes.

areas. For many centuries, however, settled lives were not necessarily any easier than hunting and gathering. Tilling, sowing, weeding, and harvesting were backbreaking labor, and the failure of a crop was a constant threat.

Archeologists have excavated sites occupied by early agriculturists at numerous places around the world. The most significant centers of farming developed in southwestern Asia, in what are now Iran, Iraq, Israel, Jordan, Syria, and Turkey; in Thailand in Southeast Asia; along the Nile River in Egypt; and in southeast Europe along the Danube River. Other early centers of agriculture have been identified along the Huang He, or Yellow River, in China; in the Indus River valley of India and Pakistan; and in the Oaxaca Valley of Mexico. Some archeologists once believed that the parallel development of agriculture in numerous places suggested that some contact existed to transmit knowledge of the new techniques around the world; today, most experts see the parallels as coincidence and believe that cultures developed their own forms of agriculture simultaneously.

Settlements

Neolithic farmers generally lived in small houses of sunbaked mudbrick or of reeds and wood, grouped into small villages that were often surrounded by wooden palisades for protection. Such communities were shaped entirely by the need to produce enough food to support themselves and their livestock from harvest to harvest. As they improved the yield of their crops over a long period of time, they began to produce surplus crops. The parallel improvement in storage methods for oil and grain—in jars, cisterns, silos, and bins of various types—allowed the population of settlements to grow. The surplus food also allowed some people to stop farming and follow more specialized professions as priests, say, or bureaucrats, craftspeople, or traders. Growing settlements and increasingly specialized labor led eventually to the emergence of the first cities, such as Jericho, founded around 9000 B.C.E. Adequate food supplies, storage, and trade supported the emergence of sophisticated urban civilizations in Mesopotamia—modern Iraq—northern India, Egypt, and Rome. Among the world's most notable cities, in the order of their development, were Thebes, Memphis, Babylon, Nineveh, Susa, Tyre, Carthage, and Jerusalem.

Markets, barter, money, and trade

The early urban civilizations were characterized by the close connection of economics with the notion of housekeeping. Production was concerned with basic household needs—food, warmth, clothing, cleanliness, and furniture—and generally took place within the household itself. Labor was provided either by members of a household or, in larger establishments or large-scale public projects such as irrigation schemes, by slaves. The forced labor of slaves was essential to the economy and society of many ancient civilizations. The ancient Mesopotamian, Indian,

BELOW: This reconstruction of an Iron Age farm in England shows how wheat fields used to surround farms to provide food and a surplus that could be traded.

The coming of cities

Over the course of more than a millennium the semipermanent villages of the first Neolithic agriculturalists developed into settlements that are recognizable as the forerunners of modern cities. Before 6000 B.C.E. Çatal Hüyük in Anatolia had grown into a community of around 5,000 people. The process of urbanization carried on over millennia in different parts of the world. In Sumer, in what is now Iraq, the development of irrigation enabled large-scale farming that supported the emergence of cities such as Eridu, Uruk, and later, Babylon. In the Indus Valley of northern India and Pakistan Mohenjo-daro and Harappa emerged between 3500 B.C.E. and 2500 B.C.E.

Archeological excavations reveal that many early cities shared similar characteristics. Many were walled for protection; they also housed large-scale religious or public buildings. Some display gridlike street plans or are divided into carefully delineated areas: for ceremonial use, for housing, and for various crafts and small-scale industries.

All early cities were dominated by agriculture, and food production and storage were their chief priority. Labor became increasingly specialized, however, as a growing market made it possible for people to exchange their specialties for other types of goods or services. An artisan class made luxury craft goods or worked with metals. Merchants organized trade that might be conducted over relatively large distances. Obsidian, or volcanic glass, from Çatal Hüyük has been found as far distant as Jericho, 500 miles away. Other classes of citizens emerged. At the top of the hierarchy were the chiefs, rulers, and bureaucrats who administered the community; at the next level the priestly class was responsible for the correct observance of religious rituals; a warrior class defended settlements from the often very real threat of attack by neighbors or rivals. Beneath the merchant and artisan classes lay a vast underclass of serfs or slaves—either captives from wars or their descendants—who performed most manual and menial labor.

Increasing specialization and division of labor, as the classical economist Adam Smith pointed out in the 18th century, led to increased production. Throughout the world urban centers came to act as focuses for increased economic activity, providing ready markets for the exchange of goods and services and thus stimulating production.

and Chinese civilizations employed slaves domestically in homes and shops or in gangs for construction or agriculture. The ancient Egyptians used slaves to build their royal palaces and the pyramids.

The widespread use of unwaged labor meant that there was no need for price and wage policies. With production and consumption centered on the household, there was no need for a theory of prices; with slaves there was no need for a theory of wages. The science of economics therefore remained little studied, even by intellectually inquisitive societies such as the ancient Greeks.

Settlement and trade

The general pattern of urban settlement that emerged comprised larger cities surrounded by the agricultural land that supported them and perhaps allied to a network of outlying smaller urban centers. The bulk of commerce was restricted to local markets, and most trading involved foodstuffs and clothing. Most people spent the bulk of their resources on food, and what they neither grew nor gathered themselves they obtained through trade.

Transporting commodities over any significant distance was an expensive and risky enterprise. Nevertheless, from Neolithic times onward international commerce and trading were an important part of the economy. In northern Europe, for example, there was a widespread trade in flint, the key material for making axes and weapons. High-quality flint was mined in extensive shafts and galleries in

ABOVE: *The ruins of Çatal Hüyük, excavated on the Konya Plain in Turkey.*

Grimes Graves in England and in Spiennes in Belgium. The flint from these mines, as well as from many open-air "factory" sites, was turned into flaked or polished axes that were traded across Europe. The axes made possible the tremendous forest clearance that made Europe an agricultural continent. The trade in such items, archeologists believe, probably took place thanks to extended series of short-range transactions between peoples who lived relatively close to one another.

Materials for practical tools were not the only traded commodity. The Bronze Age societies that emerged to dominate Europe from about 2000 until about 700 B.C.E. generally consisted of warlike groups that set great store in conspicuous display. Richly decorated weapons and shields and colored, intricate jewelry proclaimed the wealth and status of their owners. An important trade developed in luxury items such as semiprecious stones.

Copper and tin for making bronze were also much sought after. Tin ores in particular were traded great distances from their sources in Anatolia and in western and southwestern Europe. Long-distance trade flourished, with bronze cast and distributed in metal ingots of standardized shape and weight.

The U.S. economist Thorstein Veblen (1857–1929) compared the "conspicuous consumption" of the Bronze Age with the ostentatious display of wealth characteristic of the so-called Gilded Age of the late-19th century in the United States.

Burials in Scandinavia

In Bronze Age Scandinavia rich people were buried in earthen barrows, or burial mounds, with costly grave goods. The Scandinavians also placed hoards of bronze objects in lakes as religious offerings, an indication of how highly they valued them. Scandinavia lacked metal deposits, however, so all its copper and tin had to be imported. In return, the Scandinavians exported Baltic amber. This translucent orange mineral, formed by fossilized tree resin, was in great demand as a luxury commodity. Archeologists have identified an "amber route" extending thousands of miles along the great rivers of eastern Europe into

ABOVE: The renowned Stonehenge monument was built in southern England by the Neolithic farmers who settled the fertile plain.

modern Russia and from the Baltic south to the Mediterranean.

Along Bronze Age trade routes arose craft centers and large fortified settlements. Control of this trade brought great economic and political power to such settlements and conferred social status on their citizens. Some areas appear to have become wealthy through acting as intermediaries in trade. One example is the Wessex Culture of southern England, which seems to have been dominated by warrior-chiefs whose tombs, in circular barrows or mounds, are particularly rich in grave goods of gold, bronze, and amber.

A varied cargo

A striking indication of the extent of Bronze Age trade comes from the wreck of a 14th-century-B.C.E. Phoenician ship that was excavated in the 1980s off Cape Uluburun, in southern Turkey. Archeologists established that the ship was carrying ingots of copper, as well as a remarkable array of objects. The copper had been mined in Cyprus, and the tin probably came from Afghanistan. More exotic raw materials included ingots of blue glass, which the Mycenaeans used for jewelry; a ton of resin from the terebinth tree for making perfume; logs of Egyptian ebony for making luxury furniture; and quantities of unworked elephant and hippopotamus ivory. The ship's passengers seem to have included specialized merchants, as suggested by finds of weights and a wooden writing tablet, perhaps to note deals. The finds include Mycenaean, Cypriot, Canaanite, Kassite, Egyptian, and Assyrian objects, and the personal possessions of the crew were equally cosmopolitan.

A trading power

Lying between the empires of Egypt and the Hittites, Phoenicia—modern Lebanon—was the leading land and sea trading nation of the Mediterranean from around the 16th to the 4th centuries B.C.E. Phoenicians were also famous as producers of a much sought-after purple dye and timber from the famous cedar groves of Lebanon. Phoenician sailors began by sailing the eastern Mediterranean but appear to have developed methods of navigation by using the North Star, which enabled them to extend their voyages beyond Mediterranean waters. Signs of Phoenician influence have been found on the southwest coast of India and in Sri Lanka, where mariners were probably sent via the Red Sea on a trading commis-

sion. The Phoenicians also founded the city of Gades (present-day Cádiz) on the Atlantic coast of Spain. In about 600 B.C.E., according to the Greek historian Herodotus, the Egyptian pharaoh Necho commissioned Phoenicians to sail clockwise around Africa to see if it was a viable alternative trade route to the Red Sea. Evidence suggests that the expedition did indeed circumnavigate the 22,900-mile coastline of Africa.

In the seventh century B.C.E. the Phoenicians established a new capital on the North African coast at Carthage, in modern Tunisia. Gaining control of the straits of Gibraltar, at the entrance to the Mediterranean Sea, they discovered the Atlantic islands of Madeira, the Canaries, and the Azores. In the 5th century B.C.E. an expedition commanded by Himilco followed the coast of France north and crossed the English Channel to Cornwall, the source of the tin in which Phoenicians had been trading as intermediaries for years. Another expedition, led by Hanno, took an estimated 30,000 colonists on a journey southward down the Atlantic coast of Africa. The pioneers established six colonies and exploring the Senegal and Gambia rivers, and the coast south to Sierra Leone or Cameroon.

The end of Phoenicia

In the 4th century B.C.E. Greek sailors began to challenge Phoenician dominance in the Mediterranean. Phoenicia entered a long decline that ended in 146 B.C.E. when Rome destroyed Carthage at the end of the Punic Wars. In the service of the Roman Empire, however, Arab mariners revived the Red Sea trade in the early centuries of the modern era (*see* box, page 15). Using the seasonal monsoon winds,

BELOW: An example of conspicuous consumption from the Bronze Age: a bronze bracelet decorated with disks of enamel and colored glass.

LEFT: Cedar of Lebanon, important to the Phoenicians for trade and for shipbuilding.

BELOW: Phoenician trading vessels, like this one illustrated in a carving from the first century, sailed around the African coast in the sixth century B.C.E.

Arab dhows sailed down the Persian Gulf from Siraf and Hormuz as far as the East African coast, and also crisscrossed the Indian Ocean, carrying spices, sugar, aromatic woods, ships' timber, gold, ivory, copper, tin, porcelain, silk, horses, and even elephants.

Another notable example of long-distance commerce was the Silk Road between China and imperial Rome, first established around 100 B.C.E. when the Han dynasty of China made much of Central Asia safe for caravan traffic (*see* box, page 16). Goods conveyed over such vast distances in the Roman Empire tended to be luxury items, traded on through intermediaries rather than remaining with a single merchant for the whole length of the route. As Rome eventually lost its power, political upheavals along the overland routes after the fifth century C.E. curtailed the trade, but it periodically revived during periods of peace. Roman influence thus spread far beyond the considerable boundaries of the Empire. Roman goods have been found as far east as India and as far west as Ireland; goods of Indian origin were discovered in the ruins of Pompeii, the Roman city destroyed by a volcanic eruption in 79 C.E.

Money and coins

In the earliest societies goods and services were obtained by barter, or the exchange of one commodity for another. Property, such as cows or sheep, could also be used for money, but this form of exchange was cumbersome and inconvenient. From very early times, therefore, societies began to use metals as a form of exchange: metal was scarce, portable, and generally acceptable for all transactions, the basic requirements of a monetary system. In East Asia silver was the principal metal used in trade. Cast in ingots, it was marked with inscriptions giving the name of the merchant and indicating the denomination and purity of the metal. In Europe and the Middle East pieces of both gold and silver were widely used in trade as a form of exchange. Their value was determined by their weight, which had to be tested, together with the purity of the metal, every time they changed hands.

The first coins

The first true coins appeared in the kingdom of Lydia in Asia Minor sometime around 600 B.C.E. The Lydians, at that time an important industrial and trading society, began to shape electrum, a naturally occurring alloy of gold and silver, into bean-shaped lumps of fixed weight and purity and stamp them with official symbols. By 550 B.C.E. the practice of striking coins was established in the world's important trading cities. Such money was genuine commodity money, with a value determined by its metallic content. Monarchs, aristocrats, cities, and institutions began making money stamped with an identifying mark to prove its authenticity and the coin's metallic value.

The value of some early coins was remarkably stable: the drachma issued by Athens from the 6th century B.C.E. had a fairly constant content of 65 to 67 grains of fine silver. The round copper Chinese qian, introduced in the 4th century, remained a standard coin for 2,000 years. The fact that coins actually contained gold or silver, however, made it tempting for people to adulterate them. Issuing authorities were prone to debasing coinage by reducing its content of precious metal. Unscrupulous coin holders often clipped or shaved pieces off coins for their gold and silver.

Classical Greece

From the fifth century B.C.E. Greek city-states such as Athens, Corinth, and Sparta flourished. Historians know more about how the Greeks organized their economic life than about any other civilization before them. The basic industry of Greece was agriculture, the producing unit was the household, and the labor force was largely made up of slaves. Ancient cities were thus not economic centers in the modern sense of the word, involving production and industry. In the 18th century David Hume (1711–1776) pointed out that no ancient source records a city's growth as the result of the establishment of manufacturing.

Most material goods were probably bought with the rents and exactions of absen-

tee landlords living in the city, and were sold on to pay for the products of the farms and vineyards. Urban revenue also came in the form of taxes, which were in turn used to pay for produce. In Athens the silver mines of Laureum provided state revenue.

Plato and Aristotle

The ancient Greeks were some of the first people to leave a record of their political and moral thinking. The philosophers Plato (428–348 B.C.E.) and Aristotle (384-322 B.C.E.) both wrote about the problems of wealth, property, and trade. Both commentators were prejudiced against commerce and declared

ABOVE: Traders from Crete, shown in a later artist's impression. The Minoan civilization of the island traded throughout the eastern Mediterranean.

are in modern economies. The Greco-Roman world, as well as the ancient empires of the Middle East and East Asia, used a considerable amount of capital goods in the form of tools and equipment for the production of textiles, pottery, glassware, and other items sold in international markets.

The economy in Aristotle's Greece, however, operated almost entirely at the household level, so most lending and borrowing was for personal needs, rather than to generate income through investment or business. Interest was seen therefore, not in its modern context as a production cost, but rather as a charge by the more favored on the unfortunate or unwise. Like slavery, interest was treated as a problem of ethics. Aristotle condemned the charging of interest as an unworthy exaction from the less fortunate arising from the possession of money by the more fortunate. Such a position remained common well over a thousand years later during the European Middle Ages, when Catholic teaching also condemned charging interest as usury; even today, someone who charged interest on a loan to a friend would be widely condemned.

LEFT: This Celtic coin, found in France, bears the portrait of a tribal chieftain as a guarantee of its authenticity. Its irregular shape might be a result of how it was stamped, but might also reflect that it has been shaved by forgers.

that to live by trade was undesirable. They also considered labor demeaning because virtually all labor was performed by slaves. Aristotle indicated the fundamental place of slavery in the Greek economy when he included his discussion of economics only as part of a general consideration of the ethics of slavery, which he approved. Since no wages were paid for labor, the Greeks could have no view of how wages were determined.

Nor could Greek thinkers have a view about charging interest on capital, or loans, which were not used in the way in which they

The larger economy

Aristotle also raised the question of fair or just prices, which was to remain a central concern of economic thought for the next 2,000 years,

LEFT: This Roman villa—preserved when a volcanic eruption buried the city of Pompeii in 79 C.E.—would once have stood at the center of an agricultural estate that supported its own community of slaves and serfs.

although in a world without wages and interest there was no theory of price in any modern sense. The Greeks also raised the question of the larger organizing or motivating force in the economy. Plato imagined a state as an economic entity of various occupations and professions necessary for civilized life, presided over by guardians who must never "acquire homes or lands or moneys of their own [or] they will become housekeepers and husbandmen instead of guardians." While individual citizens could indulge in free enter-prise, in other words, their social governors must work at all times for the public good.

Roman economics

The Romans borrowed their economic ideas from the Greeks and had the same contempt for trade. Despite that, however, Roman trade routes reached as far as India and China, and extended throughout the empire. Roman literary works such as the *Satyricon* show that money was important in everyday life and an important concern for Roman thinkers

Early Arab traders

As early as the seventh century C.E. traders from Arabia were making direct ocean voyages from the Red Sea to the Indian subcontinent. Such voyages were made possible by the Arabs' use of the dhow, a highly adaptable boat rigged with a triangular lateen sail, and by their understanding of the seasonal monsoon winds of the Indian Ocean. The southwest monsoon aided the outward voyage from July to October, and the northeast monsoon powered the return trip from November to March. The dhows carried aromatic spices, pearls, and fine textiles, as well as bulk commodities such as rice, metals, and even horses. Timber for shipbuilding was imported to Arab lands that lacked forests.

Arab trade was also brisk along the eastern coast of Africa. In the winter season dhows carrying goods from the Persian Gulf sailed in the lee of the Hadhramaut on the Arabian Sea before running south with the northeast monsoon wind. Arab trade with the East African kingdoms from Mogadishu to Mozambique included gold, ivory, and slaves. Arab slave traders founded an important trading station at Zanzibar, where their descendants, the Shirazi, still form a distinctive people. Arab trade routes were also an important conduit for the spread of religion as the merchant class of East Africa became increasingly Islamicized and used the same routes to make pilgrimages to Mecca.

ABOVE: *Easily maneuverable and capable of sailing long distances, the dhow, like this example painted in the early 20th century off the coast of East Africa, allowed Arab traders to master the waters of the Arabian and Indian Oceans.*

The Silk Road

The Silk Road was one of the most important and extensive trade routes of the ancient world. The 4,000-mile-long road, which was actually a caravan route rather than a paved road, joined the civilizations of Rome and China. From Sian in China it ran northwest across deserts and through mountains into Afghanistan and from there to the Levant, the east coast of the Mediterranean, where goods were loaded onto ships for Rome.

As was characteristic of ancient trade routes, few merchants traveled the whole length of the Silk Road. Goods were handled by a series of intermediaries. The goods included Chinese silk—a valued commodity at a time when no Europeans knew how to make silk—and Roman wool and precious metals. Traders also shipped many other high-value commodities from intermediate points in India and Arabia.

With the loss of Roman territory in Asia and growing Arab dominance of the Levant, the route became dangerous and was less used. It was revived under the Mongols in the 13th and 14th centuries, when the Venetian Marco Polo used it to travel to China.

ABOVE: *A trade caravan crosses one of the desert sections of the Silk Road.*

Like Aristotle, the Romans granted moral superiority to farming, idealizing the farmer as self-sufficient, resourceful, and hard-working and thus superior to the town dweller. The stereotype has endured almost to the present. Although Rome probably originated as a rural society of independent farmers, its later agriculture developed along lines that had little to do with the stereotype. In the early centuries of the current era agriculture took on an almost capitalistic character. The large estates that supplied grain to the empire were owned by absentee landowners and cultivated mainly by slave labor under the supervision of hired overseers.

The estates that dominated Roman agrarian life from the beginning of the common era resembled medieval manors in their scale and organization. Roman estates centered on the big house, or villa, of the owner, surrounded by outbuildings: kitchen, bakery, brewhouse, workshops, stables, barns, and cellars. Most of the laborers were established in separate quarters, called a village, although sometimes the latter was no bigger than a hamlet. The land might be divided into that part cultivated for the master, that tilled for the sustenance of the peasants, and the meadows, pasture, woodland, and wasteland that were not in cultivation but which provided firewood, animal fodder, vegetable products, and so on for the estate to be nearly self-sustaining.

The growth of serfdom

As slaves, usually war captives, decreased in number, tenant farmers—who were sometimes freed slaves themselves—took their place on Roman estates. Slaves and tenants alike were forced to work on a fixed schedule; tenants paid a predetermined share of their produce to the estate owner. A third-century imperial edict intended to encourage agriculture decreed that all cultivators of the soil, and their heirs after them, must remain on their lands. In return, however, they could not have their lands taken away from them, even if they were slaves. Under this system the great landowners controlled the *coloni*, or settlers on their lands, whether free or in bondage. They held economic and often total power as landlords. By the fourth century many tenants had fallen into serfdom and were tied to the land and its owner.

Seigneurialism

When German invaders conquered the Western Roman Empire in the fifth century, they took over the system of estates farmed by dependent cultivators. In England and the rest of northern Europe seigneurialism, or feudalism, was introduced by powerful nobles or by the Catholic Church. The word *seigneurialism* derives from the Roman peasants who had their own part of an estate to farm but still relied on the senior, or "old man." Small freeholders continued to exist, but more and more of them found it desirable to "commend" themselves to the care of lords.

From the sixth century Europe suffered a breakdown of strong central government that accelerated the development of the seigneurial estate as the principal unit of local political authority. The absence of strong urban settlements meant that economies were largely localized, which also strengthened the power of the seigneur. All the people under the jurisdiction of the seigneur were under his care and protection, in return for which they were obliged to be judged and punished by him and directed by him in their work. They were his serfs, a term that became common after the 10th century.

The greatest of Europe's medieval rulers, Charlemagne, who established a Frankish empire that covered much of the western continent, consolidated his power by allying members of the landholding class to him by special oaths of loyalty, rewarded by grants of land. This linkage of ties of personal dependence with political power is characteristic of the social system called feudalism. The vassals of the king, his dependents, and their vassals in turn became surrogates of the king himself.

The monasteries

Inseparable from Charlemagne's military and political consolidation of his empire was his growing sense that he had a Christian mission. The emperor founded monastic houses in border territories that served as pioneer establishments, bringing forests and marshlands under cultivation. In the ninth century, however, new migrations and invasions—the Vikings from the north, Islamic sea raiders

known as Saracens from the Mediterranean, and the Magyars from Hungary—weakened the great European expansion Charlemagne had inspired. Land ceased to be cultivated, populations declined, trade was disrupted, and travel over even short distances became dangerous because of bandits. The monasteries once again became outposts of civilization.

ABOVE: This artist's re-creation shows Charlemagne, king of the Franks and Holy Roman emperor, on his throne. The emperor encouraged an expansion of European economic activity and influence.

Trade routes

The Vikings, Saracens, and Magyars were gradually defeated or settled down in the 100 years from 950 to 1050. Europe then enjoyed a period of settled population that coincided with a period of significant population growth. Towns expanded, challenging the tendency of medieval farms toward economic self-sufficiency by including them in a wider economic network. Trade and commerce, particularly in Italy and southern France and in the Low Countries, increased in quantity, regularity, and extent.

Commerce expanded gradually during the 12th and 13th centuries. Long-distance trade became safer once merchants began to form associations for the protection of travelers abroad. The main long-distance trade routes were from the Baltic and the eastern Mediterranean to central and northern Europe. From the forests of the Baltic came raw materials: timber, tar, furs, and skins. Slaves were also an important commodity. From the East came luxury goods: spices, jewelry, and textiles. In exchange western Europe exported raw materials and processed goods.

The feudal system

From about 1000 until the arrival of the pandemic known as the Black Death in the 1340s, seigneurialism dominated Europe. Seigneurs had varying degrees of wealth and power, and their estates were of different sizes, but they were all rulers, employers, and patriarchs, dominating the lives of the peasants. From each peasant the lord had the right to so many days' labor each week and so many extra days during plowing, harvest, and other special times. He also had the right to his serfs' military service during military campaigns. A feudal lord might build mills, ovens, or winepresses and require his serfs to use them and to pay him to do so.

In general, a lord had the right to impose an annual poll or head tax from the serfs on his estate, to tax their income, to take an inheritance tax at their deaths, and to reclaim their lands if they died without heirs. In return, the peasants, even those of low origins, had the right to hold their land and pass it on to their descendants. Although a lord might be able to give away or sell them and their descendants like possessions, he also had to give or sell their lands with them. The peasants not only had certain strips of arable

BELOW: A 12th-century monarch watches over the operations of his exchequer, or treasury, as officials weigh coins as payment for waiting soldiers.

land to farm in the open fields of their villages, but they also enjoyed grazing rights on the common pastures and rights to gather fuel and building materials in the common woodland and wasteland.

The three-field system

Agriculture in the Middle Ages benefited from a number of significant changes. In particular, many communities adopted the so-called three-field system. Arable land was divided into huge fields that were in turn split into long, thin strips allocated to the seigneur or to individual peasants and their families. To allow soil to recover after growing a crop, villages had previously had two fields, one of which they sowed each season, but one of which they left fallow. In the three-field system, however, only a third of the land, rather than half, remained fallow. Another third was planted in fall with wheat, barley, or rye; in the spring the remaining third was planted with oats, barley, and legumes for a harvest in late summer. The system had numerous benefits. The legumes—peas and beans—helped the soil replenish its nitrogen and provided variety in people's diet; growing a surplus of oats allowed the increased use of horses as draft animals; above all, improved plowing allowed peasants to double their crop yield.

The economic basis of seigneurialism in Europe was challenged by the gradual reappearance of a market economy, characterized by private ownership, trade, and individual decision-making about what to produce and sell. Peasants who were producing surplus crops were now able to sell them for money and to buy freedoms of various sorts from

The Viking economy

ABOVE: *Warriors' shields lashed to its sides, the Viking longboat was a feared sight in coastal communities throughout northern Europe.*

From the 800s to the 1000s northern Europe was dominated by the Vikings of Scandinavia. From their homelands on the North and Baltic Seas the Norsemen, as they were also known, used their seafaring and boat-building skills to build a maritime empire. Feared in coastal communities as warlike raiders, the Vikings were also adventurous explorers and traders who opened trade routes around Europe's coasts and along its rivers. Their trade routes stretched from the Baltic to the Black Sea and Constantinople (now Istanbul), via the Dnepr River, and to the Caspian Sea, Persia, and the East and Far East, via the Volga River. Norwegians ventured north to Iceland and Greenland, and reached North America in about 1030. The Vikings sailed up the Seine River to occupy much of northern France and navigated the western seaboard of Europe to enter the Mediterranean. They founded great cities, including Dublin in Ireland, York in England, Novgorod and Smolensk in Russia, and Kiev in Ukraine.

Originally farmers, the Nordic peoples adapted as their control of international trade grew. In northern Europe they traded wool, salted fish, furs, and sealskins, and enjoyed a virtual monopoly on ivory. Walrus tusks from Greenland and Iceland provided the material for most medieval ivory artefacts.

Further south the Vikings offered an alternative route to the Mediterranean, much of which was then under Islamic control, . From the north came slaves, furs, walrus ivory, ropes, and honey; from the south, in return, came wine, spices, and silks. The Volga route, which was more heavily used for trading than the Dnepr, was controlled by the Bulgars and the Kazakhs, who had close

ABOVE: *This so-called horn of plenty, buried with a rich Viking in Sweden, contains the precious belongings, including coins, of the dead man.*

contacts with the caliphate of Baghdad. Arab merchants from the south and east traveled to buy goods and slaves from the Vikings, paying in gold or more often silver. Such was the value of the trade that in the late 10th century the silver mines of the caliphate of Baghdad were exhausted, and Germany became the main source of the metal.

their lords. The latter used the money to hire wage labor in the fields or mercenary armies for war. The system of two classes, lords and peasants, was also undermined by rising towns whose bourgeoisie represented a middle class between the two. The Black Death of the later Middle Ages effectively struck the death blow to the seigneurial system. As Europe's population fell, labor became so valuable that in order to keep their land under cultivation and yielding revenue, few lords could afford to refuse their peasants extended rights to farm on their own behalf.

The Black Death

The Black Death as a form of plague carried by fleas that lived on rats. The disease probably originated in the steppes of Central Asia before spreading to China and India, and was probably carried to the Middle East and the Mediterranean by merchants traveling along established trade routes. The sickness reached Constantinople in 1347; it came to Italy, Spain, and France the next year, and Switzerland, Austria, Germany, the Low Countries, and England only a year later. In 1350 it arrived in Scandinavia and Poland. Historians estimate that Europe's population fell by about 40 percent between 1348 and 1377.

The dramatic fall in population had an immediate impact. The surplus of agricultural labor was eliminated, some villages became depopulated and eventually disappeared, and several towns declined, while much marginal land remained uncultivated. In the decades that followed, wages rose and landlords' rents fell, an illustration of the law of supply and demand that indicates difficulty in finding tenants and laborers. For those who survived these mortality crises wages were higher and food prices lower a century after the Black Death than they had been before 1347.

Monasticism

Late medieval Europe was dominated by the beliefs of Christianity and the institutions of the Roman Catholic Church. The church, with the pope as its head, controlled large parts of central and northern Italy, and was a powerful force throughout Europe through the administration of justice in church courts. Monasteries and other religious houses, as in Charlemagne's time, were not just important spiritual centers but were also thriving economic centers, acting as landowners, producers of wine or produce, and trading places.

Well organized and technologically innovative, for example, the new Cistercian order was by the 12th century making a substantial contribution to economic life. Cistercian monks were influential in the development of techniques for reclaiming wasteland and clearing forest for farming. They also excelled in producing and marketing grain and wool.

Religion and usury

The teachings of Christianity had a great influence on economic life and theory. Christian doctrine tended to condemn elements of business that are considered essential in modern economies. The economic ideas of the Roman Catholic church were expressed in the canon law, which regarded commerce as morally inferior to agriculture. Jesus's compassion for the poor and his associated disapproval of financial institutions were summed up in his

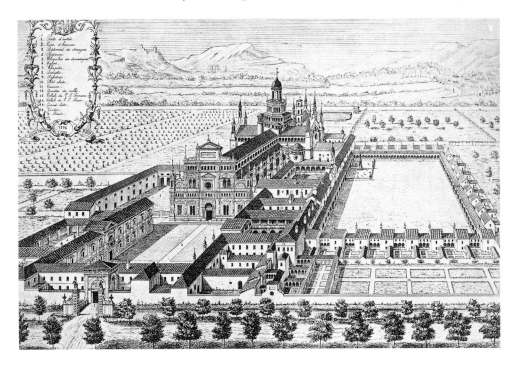

LEFT: Monasteries, like this one founded at Pavia, Italy, in the 14th century, acted as economic centers in many parts of rural Europe. As well as places for buying and selling, monasteries were also conduits for the dissemination of knowledge of, for example, new farming techniques.

LEFT: This illustration from 1349 shows victims of the Black Death in Norway. Animals, as well as humans, fell victim to the disease.

attack on the moneylenders in the temple. To contemporary theologians, therefore, the Bible cast suspicion on even the possession of riches, although both the church and the religious orders amassed land and wealth.

The canon law condemned usury, or the charging of interest on loans, and the condemnation had a considerable effect on commerce. Like Aristotle, Christian teaching saw interest as an exaction by the fortunate on the needy and therefore morally reprehensible. There was still a need for financial capital, however. Rulers needed funds to fight wars, for example. One source was Europe's Jews. Discriminatory laws in many countries prevented non-Christians from owning land. This encouraged substantial Jewish involvement in medieval banking and commerce, neither of which were condemned in Jewish scripture.

The association of Jews with moneylending led to their victimization, especially during the Crusades, a series of campaigns by Europe's Christian rulers against the Islamic peoples of the Middle East. Thousands of Jews were massacred in the upsurge of feeling against non-Christians. In the 13th and 14th centuries several European monarchs filled their treasuries by confiscating Jewish property and expelling its owners. In 1290 Edward I expelled the English Jews; Charles VI of France followed in 1394. As Europe's economy took on a more modern shape, it proved merciless for many Europeans.

Beyond Europe

Trade brought Europeans into contact with peoples outside the continent. In the Middle East they had close contacts with the Islamic world. The economy of Islam thrived: Arab traders controlled the lucrative trade routes across the Sahara in Africa, importing gold and slaves to the Middle East, and traded by sea with India. The Ottoman Turks controlled the overland routes with East Asia.

The greatest single empire in the period from 500 to 1500 lay in China, where a feudal system had operated for more than 2,000 years. By the 11th century c.e., under the Tang and Song dynasties, China had developed a sophisticated economy, with paper money and emerging forms of banking. The Chinese also made technological advances, with inventions such as the wheelbarrow. The 13th-century Venetian traveler Marco Polo marveled at such achievements when he visited the court of the great Mongol emperor Kublai Khan in China. To demonstrate the might of the Chinese empire, Admiral Zheng He captained seven voyages between 1405 and 1434, visiting the major ports in the China Sea and the Indian Ocean, reaching as far as East Africa. In the mid–15th century, however, China gave up looking outward, and its influence disappeared from the world stage.

Of the civilizations of Southeast Asia historians know little before the Islamic conquest of the region in the 15th century. The peoples who built monuments such as Angkor Wat, in modern Cambodia, also built great irrigation works to grow the rice on which they depended. On the other side of the world, in Mesoamerica, early peoples were equally dependent on their harvests of corn. Great religious centers grew up, linked by wide trading networks and characterized by highly skilled craft-making.

SEE ALSO:

• Volume 1, page 6: What is money?

• Volume 2, page 6: An introduction to business

• Volume 5, page 43: Goods and services

• Volume 5, page 52: Interest

• Volume 5, page 57: Labor

• Volume 5, page 110: Trade and international trade

The emergence of Europe

At the dawn of the early modern world Europe was eclipsed by the cultural and technological achievements of other civilizations in Africa, China, Japan, India, and the Near East. By the 17th century, however, Europe had emerged to dominate the economy of the globe.

LEFT: Salt is carefully weighed and distributed in this illustration from late 14th century Italy. As an essential commodity, salt was often subject to strict government controls in early modern Europe.

Around the 12th century, at the height of the Middle Ages, life in Europe in many ways followed the same patterns it had for the previous three centuries. There were few countries with established borders; indeed, the word Europe itself was rarely used. The continent's tiny educated elite perceived Europe as "Christendom," a religious rather than geographical entity that united them under the authority of the Roman Catholic Church. Centralized government was emerging but remained weak. The social and economic structure in much of the continent reflected the feudal system, a network of privileges and duties whose roots ultimately lay in land ownership and military service.

For most people life remained the same series of struggles their forebears had faced, from growing enough food to eat to building houses that remained standing, and tradition

LONDON.

ABOVE: *In 1488, when this map was published, London had become by far England's most populous city and was a thriving center of trade thanks in particular to its outstanding river and sea communications.*

was an important part of the economic system. Beneath such apparent continuity, however, life was changing. Trading activity intensified; a gradual movement began of peasants from the countryside to Europe's urban centers, which grew more important in the economic and political landscape; government became more centralized, with strong monarchies establishing bureaucracies and tax systems. In some ways money became more important than status in shaping the relationships between individuals.

The feudal system declines

At the heart of the changes in European life lay the evolution of the feudal system, the continent's main form of social organization from the eighth century onward. The term describes a system under which all land was owned by lords who permitted their vassals to live on it in return for their labor and, when required, military service. In the feudal system the majority of people were farmers and serfs who were tied to the estate where they were born and remained subject to the will of their lord. On their side lords had an obligation to protect the peasants and serfs on their estates. Because the European economy remained profoundly agricultural—the vast majority of people were either employed directly in farming or stock raising or in associated trades such as weaving, dyeing, and brewing—feudalism was an economic as well as a social system, making each lord's estate largely self-supporting.

The Black Death

The fundamental cause of the changes in feudalism was population change. In the mid–14th century a plague called the Black Death killed between a third and a half of the continent's population (*see* page 20). The survivors could barely plant or harvest their crops. Whole towns were deserted. Labor was in such short supply that peasants who had once been tied to their lands could now hire their services to the highest bidder.

The effects of the Black Death accelerated processes that were already taking place in European society. Feudal tributes, by which serfs gave their labor in return for a lord's protection of their welfare, were gradually being replaced by money wages; some serfs formally leased farms from their landlords. Such innovations prepared the ground for the emergence of a society in which there were no serfs or bondsmen, and in which a cash system would replace many feudal duties.

Urban Europe

Europe's towns and cities grew increasingly important. Cities such as London, Paris, and Lübeck emerged as thriving centers of population and trade, where people could receive an education or work in trade, crafts, or other employment in return for cash. Labor tended to become more specialized, as people followed one particular trade, knowing that they could buy what goods they did not produce themselves. Such opportunities attracted a constant stream of peasants from the countryside before and after the Black Death. Some of the new arrivals flourished; others found themselves part of a growing underclass of unemployed poor, no longer enjoying the protection of a feudal lord. Contemporaries became ever more aware of the begging and crime that characterized much of the period.

The more towns and cities grew, the more they offered opportunities for trade and manufacture as well as a market for agricultural produce. As centers prospered, their citizens began to strive for political self-determination. Wealthy merchants who no longer wished to be dominated by the interests of the feudal aristocracy established town councils that reflected their own concerns. In what is today Germany a number of free towns emerged, acknowledging no political authority other than that of their own leading citizens.

Towns and cities brought new forms of social organization. Craftspeople founded guilds that, like early labor unions, protected the interests of their members. They imposed requirements for training, for example, or laid down standards for the quality of goods, thus protecting the reputation of their craft; on the other hand, they often resisted technological innovation that seemed to threaten their income and so became highly conservative forces dedicated to maintaining their own privilege. In Liège in Belgium in 1589 the cloth guild banned the introduction of a new loom that would allow weavers to produce more work, claiming that it was protecting the livelihood of its poorer members.

Economics and warfare

Other factors contributing to the decline of feudalism included changes in the nature of warfare and politics. The early modern period witnessed the slow emergence of nation-states, that is, polities with centralized government and established frontiers. The process did not happen everywhere: strong monarchies emerged in England, France, and Poland, for example, but Germany remained a collection of small independent states within the Holy Roman Empire, and the Italian peninsula was home to many fiercely independent city-states, including the republics of Venice and Florence. Such a situation, in which noble dynasties fought to become the centralized power or in which smaller states or cities clashed over, say, the control of trade, made warfare endemic in the 15th century.

In the past such wars would have been fought by armies of mounted knights accompanied by peasant footsoldiers raised by feudal lords. Increasingly, however, the coming of gunpowder weapons gave prominence to more professional armed forces rather than groups of mounted knights and feudal armies. Just as peasants chose to make monetary payments to their lords rather than undertaking labor or military service, so the lords preferred to receive money in order to pay for weapons and the better-trained troops to use them. Such soldiers fought under contracts that lasted for a specified term during which the

BELOW: The Dutch artist Jan Massys painted The Tax Collector *in 1539. The efficient collection of taxes was essential to support the increasingly centralized governments of Europe.*

European trade fairs

In the Middle Ages, particularly during the 13th and 14th centuries, the chief focus of European trade was a network of seasonal trade fairs. Merchants from the immediate area and from considerably further afield assembled perhaps for a few weeks in what took on the character of temporary towns of carts, tents, and caravans. At the end of the fair the traders took their purchases and went their various ways. Some took raw materials, such as wool, and placed them with families that turned it into cloth, which the merchant then sold at another fair. Some went to other fairs to sell their goods to other traders; others sold their stocks direct to consumers alongside the food produce that dominated the local markets that were each community's daily place of trade. In this way, by a series of transactions over relatively short distances, goods not only from Europe but also from such distant sources as East Asia or North Africa were distributed around the continent.

Many of the most important fairs clustered along the main axes of European trade, which passed roughly from Italy and the Alps in the south to the Low Countries in the north, and from France and Spain in the west to Germany and Central Europe in the East. The most famous individual fair was held at Champagne, in what is now northern France. Later, the fair at Geneva in modern Switzerland also became important. Other important fairs were held in Pavia and Milan in Italy, Frankfurt and Leipzig in Germany, and London in England. Many fairs, as well as being trade centers, maintained labor exchanges where domestic or agricultural servants could hire themselves out for a year at a time.

As the nature of business changed, trade fairs became less important in the European economy. By the 18th century permanent shops had largely replaced temporary fairs and markets as the places where goods were bought and sold. Improved transportation and communication also undermined the importance of fairs, making it easier to move commodities around the continent in larger amounts. Some fairs did survive, however: they were useful in that they concentrated trade in a single place, allowing merchants to exchange information, gauge market conditions and demand for various products, and fix competitive prices.

ABOVE: *A contemporary painting shows a cloth market in the Netherlands around 1530. Much of the wool would have originated in England and passed from fair to fair throughout continental Europe.*

troops received pay and perhaps rights to captured loot. This change marked the beginning of a transition to mercenary armies, which would dominate the next centuries.

Governments and trade

The emergence of strong dynastic monarchies in early modern Europe undermined the political dominance of other feudal lords. In some countries, including Sweden, England, and France, the aristocracy fought, sometimes violently, to retain their influence or to establish new bodies that gave them a voice in government. Another challenge to the preeminence of the landed classes came from trading cities such as Venice and Florence in Italy, Bruges in Flanders, Antwerp and Amsterdam in the Low Countries, and London in England. The rich merchants of such cities adopted the attitudes of traditional nobles, making charitable donations to religious houses, for example, or patronizing artists. They became extremely influential, not only in urban centers but throughout the whole European economy.

The importance of trade in increasing the gold and silver stocks of nation-states, usually through the taxation of merchants, meant that governments had to pay some attention at least to the needs of Europe's merchants when deciding their priorities. Some governments encouraged merchant capitalism, that is, helping merchants who invested their capital in order to accumulate further profits.

Protection and monopoly

The alliance between government and merchants was particularly important in states that lacked gold or silver mines and needed to seek other ways to accumulate wealth. Some used government control of foreign trade to maintain a surplus of exports over imports, ensuring that traders in other nations paid for goods in gold or silver. Merchants also urged governments to fix prices, for example, avoiding the likelihood of being undercut by competition. The state intervened in the economy in numerous ways. Monarchs found it advantageous to grant their supporters patents of monopoly—licences to be the sole supplier of or dealer in a particular product or in a particular part of the world—or to control the sale of goods in overseas colonies.

Monopoly—a situation in which there is a single seller of a good or service for which there is no close substitute—was particularly useful for sovereigns who were looking for

RIGHT: Martin Luther, shown in this contemporary engraving, began the Reformation that challenged the authority of the Catholic Church.

BELOW: This manuscript from 1338 shows the merchant Marco Polo leaving Venice on his trip to China in 1271. Venetian trade routes extended via the Middle East to China and Japan.

ways to maintain the flow of cash to sustain their armies, courts, and life styles. Rulers awarded charters that gave court favorites a monopoly to trade in basic essentials such as salt and tobacco; all such charters granted the sovereign an ample share of the profits. Most major European nations also granted monopoly powers to private companies to stimulate exploration and settlement in new lands. Governments thus encouraged the settlement of America and Asia without themselves risking money in the venture. The monarch's power to award monopolies led to many abuses, however, as court favorites profited at the expense of other merchants or investors.

The Reformation and wealth

The upturn in trade was paralleled by profound religious change. When the German monk Martin Luther formulated his 95 Theses in 1517, protesting abuses within the Catholic Church, the protest triggered a movement that eventually created a new form of Christianity and a division of Europe into Catholic and Protestant forms of the faith.

During the Middle Ages religious teachings, following the arguments of earlier thinkers such as the ancient Greek philosopher Aristotle and the scholar Saint Thomas Aquinas, condemned wealth and its accumulation. The church argued that the spiritual dimension of life was more important than the physical. The Catholic Church especially condemned usury, or charging interest on loans, as a sin that earned profit without labor. This effectively discouraged wealthy merchants from advancing loans to other investors.

As the Church sought to adapt to the changing economic world, however, and Catholics sought to adapt their faith to their lives, the pursuit of wealth increasingly lost its negative connotations. In 1515 a German Catholic theologian, Johann Eck, came up with a formula to reclassify loans as investment contracts on which it was permissible to make a profit. In such ways it became legitimate for Christians to finance mercantile ventures with borrowed money.

Entrepreneurs and ambition

Such changes encouraged the emergence of a figure who would remain important in later economies: the entrepreneur, or risk-taker. A key element in capitalism is the undertaking of investment or other activities in the expectation that they will yield gain in the future. Because the future is to a greater or less extent unknown, the promise of gain always comes with a risk of loss: ships full of goods might sink, for example. On a larger scale an expensive expedition to found a colonial settlement might either fail or not pay for its own

costs for a long time. Having access to funds to invest, being able to spot an opportunity for profit, and being prepared to take risks were the role of the entrepreneur.

The emergence of the entrepreneur was one sign of a more general psychological change in early modern Europe. The outlook of the medieval world had been fatalistic: a person's place in society, as much as a failed crop or the collapse of a cathedral, was ordained by God's will. Such a view made people inclined to accept their lot. Now, the decline of the feudal system and the creation of money-based societies in cities such as Florence or Amsterdam encouraged a far more interactive view of the world in which individuals could improve their lot by education or better themselves through successful trade. Through ambition and acquisitiveness people could influence their own lives.

Protestantism and capitalism

A famous theory put forward by the German economist and socialist Max Weber (1864–1920) linked the development of capitalism directly to the ethical and religious ideas of the Reformation. The Protestant emphasis on the virtues of hard work and thrift and the stress on the importance of the individual, Weber argued, meshed with capitalism's emphasis on the same qualities. Weber also argued that the prevailing philosophies in East

ABOVE: Travelers pay a toll to cross a bridge in this copy of a 15th-century cathedral window. The proliferation of tolls and customs posts made road travel highly expensive for merchants.

The Hanseatic League

ABOVE: *The quarters of the Hanseatic League in Antwerp, in Flanders, are shown in this 16th-century engraving. The league established trading enclaves in cities such as Bruges in Flanders, Bergen in Norway, Novgorod in Russia, and London, England.*

In the 15th century a federation of cities called the Hanseatic League dominated trade in northern Europe. The roots of the federation lay in modern Germany, which was then both part of the Holy Roman Empire and a patchwork of principalities seeking independence. Urban citizens used the power struggle to buy freedom from feudal obligations by paying taxes to both emperors and princely rulers. The free cities that emerged were dominated by merchants who greatly increased trade.

In the late 12th and early 13th centuries German merchants took control of trade in the Baltic Sea, forming *hanses,* or associations to guard themselves from robbers and pirates. In the late 13th century these associations grew into a league that included such towns as Lübeck and Hamburg.

The league aimed to further the interests of its members: it built numerous lighthouses, for example, and standardized weights and measures. The league also set out to organize trade by winning commercial privileges, creating enclaves abroad, and building new towns. By the 14th century the league enjoyed great prosperity from trading grain, timber, flax, and furs from Russia and Poland to Flanders and England, and cloth in return.

As powerful nation-states such as Poland-Lithuania and Muscovy formed in the 14th and 15th centuries, and as Atlantic shipping routes grew in importance, the Hansa's influence declined. By 1500 Dutch mariners had stolen the league's trade in the North Sea. In the next century the Swedes came to dominate the Baltic, and the league was effectively dead.

Asia, under the influence of religions such as Buddhism and Hinduism, prevented the simultaneous development of capitalism there, even in societies whose available resources and technological knowledge matched those of Europe. In Buddhist Japan, for example, merchants ranked very low in the social system.

Weber's theory was influential for a considerable time but no longer has popular support among historians who point out, for example, that many trades and individuals involved with a market economy failed to embrace Protestantism. Weber's theory also failed to reflect the complex nature of the Reformation. It was a far from uniform move-

ABOVE: The artist Hans Holbein painted this 1532 portrait of an unnamed merchant of the Steel Yard, the Hanseatic League's enclave in London. The portrait captures the seriousness and prudent record-keeping associated with merchants and traders.

ings—thanks to the newly introduced printing press, which allowed the publication in local or vernacular languages of religious literature formerly available only in Latin. Popular education was also stimulated through the opening of many new schools.

The development of economic tools

The availability of printed books, Protestantism's promotion of reading, and the use of vernacular languages led to a rise in literacy in much of Europe. This rise, in turn, encouraged better communications and more accurate record-keeping that made it easier for merchants to keep their accounts.

The Italian mathematician Luca Pacioli and other scholars wrote practical works to instruct merchants and traders in accounting. Pacioli invented the double-entry system of bookkeeping that is still used today; in this system every transaction is recorded twice, as a debit and a corresponding credit, usually on opposite pages of a ledger. This system allows firms to balance their books by ensuring that credits and debits come to the same total and allow the production of income and earned surplus statements.

Other works gave advice on converting currencies with different amounts of silver, calculating prices, and dividing profits among unequal investors. Such skills were highly important. Different localities used different measures of weight or length for measuring goods, and virtually every principality minted its own coins, which contained various amounts of precious metal. On a short journey in the Low Countries in the 1520s the German artist Albrecht Dürer noted that he had to deal in 18 separate currencies. New money exchanges were built where merchants could weigh and swap one type of coinage for another.

Trade improvements

Various other developments helped overcome obstacles to trade. Better ships made it easier to transport cargo by sea, avoiding slow road and river journeys that were subject to a host of tolls imposed by local principalities: there were more than 200 on the Loire River in France. The increasing power of centralized governments offered increasing protection against the bandits who plagued travelers on Europe's roads.

The greatest benefit to commerce, however, was the bill of exchange. It was an old development that replaced coins with paper bills, originally used as promises. A merchant might sell a quantity of timber to another merchant and receive in return a bill of exchange promising him or his representative a certain amount of cloth in another city or country.

ment and had widely varying results throughout western Europe. In some places the feudal nobility and the Catholic hierarchy found their power challenged by mercantile classes and monarchical rulers; in others they found their position reinforced by the new vigor with which Catholicism reacted to the new religion.

Some parts of Europe gained a greater measure of political, religious, and cultural independence as the authority of the Catholic Church was shattered. In countries such as France and modern Belgium, however, Catholicism remained dominant, although France was wracked for 60 years by the Wars of Religion, a series of bitter struggles between the Catholic monarchy and French Protestants, known as Huguenots. In England, on the other hand, a radical form of Protestantism, Puritanism, was an important factor in the civil war (1642–1649) that temporarily replaced the monarchy with a commonwealth, or republic.

In general, both the Reformation and the Catholic response, known as the Counter-Reformation, advanced national languages and literature—and therefore nationalist feel-

There was thus no need to transport bulky materials over long distances. By the 16th century such bills had become purely financial instruments not connected with the transfer of actual goods. They might be issued in one city to be repaid in another after a certain period. In effect, such notes let merchants invest in various ventures in different places without any goods changing hands at all. A financier from Flanders noted in 1543 that "one can no more trade without bills of exchange than sail without water."

European expansion

As trade grew easier, trade routes became more international. The city-states of the Italian peninsula grew rich on international commerce during the period from 1350 to 1500. Venice had extensive contacts with the Byzantine empire of the Near East, which was ruled from Constantinople (modern Istanbul). The Byzantines and their successors, the Ottoman Turks, controlled an empire that dominated the overland routes through Asia; the Venetians used such routes to build a far-reaching trade network. In the 13th century the merchant Marco Polo traveled from Venice across Asia to visit the imperial court of China. On his return Polo wrote a famous book about his travels.

Venetian sea power in the eastern Mediterranean allowed the republic to monopolize the trade in spices, transported from East Asia and the Middle East to Venice and then throughout Europe. Other Italian city-states—Genoa and Florence—were also trading powers. Their merchants and other leading citizens grew wealthy thanks to the thriving trade. Such people were the patrons of the mid–15th century revival of learning and the arts called the Renaissance; they used their money to build churches and palaces, erect statues, and commission paintings, jewelry, and tapestries.

Banking

The citizens of the Italian city-states, particularly Genoa and Florence, also led the development of banking in the 15th and 16th centuries. Supporting new ventures fell originally to merchants wealthy enough to lend money to their contemporaries. Such people emerged as merchant bankers, advancing money in return for a share of profits. Banking became more complex, and banks, which were all privately owned, accepted deposits, exchanged foreign coins for local currency, and engaged in bullion dealing of precious metals or coins made from them. The Florentine gold coin, the florin, became the standard of trade throughout Europe.

Since commerce demanded regular international transfers of money, banks became more important. Financial power brought

ABOVE: At Potosí, high in the Andes of Bolivia, the Spanish discovered what they described as a "mountain of silver," shown here in a contemporary engraving.

political influence to great banking families, such as the Medicis in Florence and the Fuggers of Augsberg. Bankers made loans to towns or to Europe's rulers. The Medicis used their influence to elect or become popes, while the Fuggers made a huge loan to Charles V of Spain in 1519 to finance his successful campaign to become Holy Roman emperor (*see* box, page 35). The heyday of the great banking dynasties lasted some 150 years. At the end of the 16th century, the monarchs of France and Spain began to default on their vast debts. Many smaller banks failed; even the mighty Fugger bank suffered badly from the losses.

The spice trade

Because Venice enjoyed a monopoly of trade with the Levant, as the eastern shore of the Mediterranean was known, it could demand exorbitant prices for goods such as spices. Pepper and cloves were luxury commodities in Europe, serving to disguise the taste of food that was sometimes rotten and always dull. Western European nations, such as Portugal and Spain, began to seek their own sea routes to the Spice Islands of modern Indonesia.

In the mid–15th century the Portuguese prince Henry the Navigator (1394–1460) founded a naval school to train sailors and to advance shipbuilding. Portuguese developments included the caravel, a sturdy sailing ship rigged so that it could advance against the wind by following a series of zigzags, a technique known as tacking. With Henry's encouragement, Portuguese navigators explored south along the west coast of Africa until 1488, when Bartolomeu Dias rounded the Cape of Good Hope at the continent's tip and reached the Indian Ocean. In 1498 Vasco da Gama became the first European to arrive by sea in India. Soon the Venetian trade with India, east Asia, and the Spice Islands, today called the Moluccas, passed into the hands of Portuguese mariners. The trade was not as lucrative as might have been expected, however. The societies the Europeans encountered had enough commodities of their own to be reluctant to trade with the newcomers.

Discovering America

In 1492 the Genoese Christopher Columbus set sail on behalf of Spain in search of a new route to the Indies. The voyage was economically motivated: Columbus was seeking a quicker route to the Spice Islands. Inspired by ancient texts and contemporary estimates that the earth was much smaller than it actually is, Columbus sailed west across the Atlantic. When he made landfall in the Bahamas, he believed that he had reached an Asian archipelago and dubbed the islands the West Indies. Over the next decades Spanish, Portuguese, and English voyagers explored the eastern coasts of North and South America, verifying the existence of huge continents.

Spain soon established colonies in the Caribbean and South America. In 1518 the Spanish conquistador Hernán Cortés landed in Mexico, where he overthrew the mighty Aztec empire. In 1532 Francisco Pizarro (1470–1541) began the conquest of Peru from its Inca rulers. The Portuguese laid claim to Brazil in 1530; the French to Canada in 1535. The first abortive English attempts to found settlements in North America—at Roanoake in 1585 and 1587—were followed by the establishment of Jamestown in Virginia in 1607.

The New World promised a rich supply of natural resources such as timber or the cod that French and English vessels fished on the Grand Banks off Newfoundland. The Spanish discovered vast reserves of silver at Potosí, in Bolivia, in the mid–1540s. At the same time, new sources of precious metals were opened in Bohemia in central Europe. Silver and gold

BELOW: *This engraving shows a 15th-century mint in the Holy Roman Empire. Craftsmen imprint the Habsburg stamp on coins, while an overseer records the currency issued.*

flooded the continent. The influx of precious metals had a profound effect on the continent's economy and its balance of power. It created more wealth and therefore more purchasing power.

A new phenomenon

Around the 16th century Europeans became aware of a new phenomenon that would remain more or less a constant of economic life, inflation, or a general increase in prices. Soon after 1500 prices began to rise quickly. Prices throughout the continent rose by an average of fourfold over the century.

Contemporary observers were more or less at a loss to explain the phenomenon. The French political theorist Jean Bodin (1530–1596), however, observed that the principal cause for "the high prices that we see today" was Europe's abundance of gold and silver. Many modern economists agree. According to the quantity theory of money formulated by U.S. economist Irving Fisher (1867–1947), for example, prices vary in direct proportion to the supply of money and the volume of trade: the more money and trade exist, the more prices rise.

At the heart of the so-called long inflation were the new sources of precious metals in the New World and Bohemia. New supplies of gold and silver greatly increased the number of coins in circulation. Spain minted treasure

ABOVE: Syrian merchants travel to Hormuz on the Persian Gulf in a book illustration from 1599. The port was the site of twice-yearly markets that represented the major terminus for trade with East Asia.

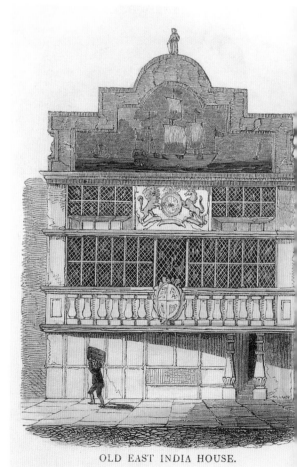

RIGHT: East India House, in London, was the early headquarters of the English East India Company. The company eventually rose to effectively rule most of the Indian subcontinent.

OLD EAST INDIA HOUSE.

into coins to pay for the military campaigns that, according to some estimates, consumed around 70 percent of its public revenues. The Spanish Habsburgs were fighting their Dutch subjects from 1554 to 1648 and later fought alongside their Austrian allies in the Thirty Years' War from 1618 to 1648. Thus Spanish coins found their way into the rest of Europe. Although the coins in circulation increased, the output of goods and services by industry and commerce did not match the rise, so money became worth less. Wages lagged behind prices, causing a steady reduction in the value of workers' income. The living standards of Europe's lower classes declined.

For merchants, meanwhile, inflation was a strong stimulative force. With rising prices there was a chance to make a profit on any durable asset that was bought for sale in the future. The differing rates of inflation in European countries further stimulated international trade.

The theory of mercantilism

As governments became preoccupied with obtaining gold and silver, and as the level of European worldwide trade increased, one of the first economic theories came into being to explain, justify, and direct the quest for monetary wealth from trade. This theory was mercantilism, which was promulgated in its heyday in the 17th century by Thomas Mun in England, Jean-Baptiste Colbert in France, and Antonio Serra in Italy.

The basic purpose of mercantile economic policy was to strengthen the national state on the understanding that this in turn would often strengthen the interests of merchants and traders, whose taxes would in turn also benefit the central government. Government regulation concentrated at least partly on creating an environment in which merchants could acquire bullion, develop agriculture and manufactures, and establish monopolies over foreign trade.

Accumulation of wealth

The most distinctive feature of mercantilism was states' preoccupation with accumulating wealth in the form of gold and silver. Such resources were necessary to ensure a nation's survival, particularly in an age of expensive bureaucracy and warfare. Because most nations did not have a natural abundance of such metals, the best way to acquire them was through a favorable balance of trade—that is, maintaining a surplus of exports over imports. Foreign states would then pay for imports in

BELOW: A sugar-cane plantation in the Antilles in the West Indies. Such large-scale agriculture, farmed by slave labor, produced new types of commodity for Europe, including not only sugar but also tobacco and, later, cotton.

gold or silver. Mercantilist states also favored low wages, believing that they would discourage imports by reducing people's ability to buy foreign goods, contribute to the export surplus, and swell the influx of gold.

From the 16th century England further reinforced its control of trade by passing a series of Navigation Acts that attempted to ensure that only English or British ships carried imports from other countries, and so only they could make profits from trade. At the height of the system, in the 17th and 18th centuries, certain goods, such as sugar, rice, and tobacco, could only be imported from Britain's colonies to British ports in British vessels. Such a move depressed trade in the colonies: the Navigation Acts were an important cause of the unrest that led to the American Revolutionary War in 1773.

As mercantilism gained importance in the 16th century, some contemporary observers protested that the real wealth of a nation lay not in its hoard of precious metals, but in its ability to develop resources or manufacture goods. To most people, however, mercantilism seemed like common sense. The more gold and silver a nation had, the richer and more powerful it was: even critics of mercantilism still made the accumulation of precious metals a priority of economic theory. It was only later that economists such as Adam Smith criticized the policy's negative effects of discouraging competition and innovation, and of bringing stagnation to weaker economies.

Domestic policies

The mercantilist concern with precious metals also affected domestic policies. Governments thought it essential to keep wages low and to ensure that the population kept growing. A large, ill-paid population produced more goods to be sold at low prices to foreigners, increasing the inward flow of money. Men, women, and children all had to work—the argument ran that the earlier children began to work, the better it was for their country's prosperity. One mercantilist thinker wrote that children of four years old should be sent to the workhouse where they would be taught to read for two hours a day and the rest of the time be kept "fully employed in any of the manufactures of the house which best suit their age, strength, and capacity." Such a policy was the inevitable consequence of a theory that saw citizens as little more than units of production for the good of their state.

Europe and the world

Following the voyages of the early navigators, European nations amassed large colonial empires in the Americas, Asia, and to a lesser

extent Africa. The level of trade with the colonies made it necessary for home countries to establish trading posts and ports, which in turn encouraged European settlement. Rare luxury imports gave way to bulkier commodities that, to be profitable, required cheap labor—to mine them, in the case of minerals, or to grow them, in the case of crops such as sugar, cotton, coffee, cocoa, tea, and tobacco.

Often Europeans forced native peoples to labor in mines or on estates called plantations.

ABOVE: A warehouse built in Venice in the 16th century by German merchants trading with the Levant.

BELOW: Luca Pacioli, the father of modern accounting, painted with a noble patron in 1495.

A banking dynasty

Even among the great families who dominated European banking in the 15th and early 16th centuries, the Fuggers of Augsberg in Germany were remarkable for their power. The European financial empire they created was the largest the western world had seen. Hans Fugger founded the dynasty in the late 14th century. His son, Jakob, became an important member of the merchants' guild, and his sons in turn expanded the family business into Venice and Rome. The youngest son, Jakob II, called the Rich (1459–1525), acquired interests in silver and copper mines and doubled the size of the company.

As financial backer of the Habsburgs of Austria and Spain, Jakob Fugger financed the campaign that won Charles V of Spain election as Holy Roman emperor in 1519. Charles also borrowed huge sums to pay for wars against the French, the Turks, and the German Protestants. Jakob died in 1525, and the business passed to his nephew Anton (1493–1560). Anton and his brothers brought the Fuggers to their peak. They were huge landowners, could mint coins, and had the powers of princes over their lands. Like the Medici, Fugger family members amassed great libraries and collections of paintings, and patronized the arts and sciences.

LEFT: Jakob Fugger II, painted by Albrecht Dürer in 1518.

When European diseases such as smallpox devastated the Native Americans, who had no natural resistance to the disease, the Europeans turned to slavery. Traders in Africa captured men and women or bought them from warring African peoples; they held them at coastal forts until they had enough cargo to fill a ship, which then sailed to the West Indies or to North America. Many slaves died on the transatlantic journey, called the Middle Passage. Those who lived were sold and set to often backbreaking work.

Shareholders and companies

New forms of commercial organization facilitated large-scale trade. Informal associations gave way to legal partnerships. When the Dutch began to establish their empire in Asia after 1600, the ships that made the lucrative voyages were owned by shareholders rather than the captains or other individuals who had previously organized the trips. Shareholding—by which investors bought shares in a vessel or in a voyage—introduced more flexibility to business. Individuals could now divide their money among ventures and their goods among ships destined for different ports. No longer was trade limited to travelers or those who could afford to build or fill a whole ship.

Shareholding was paralleled by the creation of chartered companies. These great enterprises were created by the state but were privately owned and run; they often held national monopolies over trade. The chartered company was both a business and an extension of government. The colonies of British America, for example, were established by companies chartered by the British crown to found settlements in the New World; their charters gave them both control of the trade in the region and the authority to govern it on Britain's behalf.

Numerous chartered enterprises sprang up in western Europe during the 17th and 18th centuries to further trade with the East Indies. These companies, which had varying degrees of governmental support, were chartered to acquire territory wherever they could and to exercise functions of government, including making laws, the issue of currency, the waging of war, and the administration of justice. In return, governments hoped to benefit from an increase in export trade and the accumulation of precious metals and other resources.

Power in Asia

The British East India Company received its charter from Queen Elizabeth I in 1600 and was granted a monopoly on trade in Asia, Africa, and America. It was run by a governor and 24 directors from among its stockholders. In 1610 and 1611 its first "factories," or trading posts, were established in India in Madras and Bombay. In 1689 the company began to establish administrative districts. In 1751 and 1757 Robert Clive, a company official, defeated the French East India Company—chartered

in 1664—and began a period of effective company rule that lasted until the Indian Mutiny of 1857. After this bitter uprising against company rule the British government itself formally took over rule of the subcontinent.

The Dutch government, meanwhile, had in 1602 granted the Dutch East India Company a monopoly on trade from the Cape of Good Hope east to the Strait of Magellan and sovereign rights in whatever territory it acquired. From the colonial capital the Dutch established at Batavia (now Jakarta, Indonesia) company influence spread through the Malay Archipelago and to China, Japan, India, and Iran. In 1652 the company established the first European settlement in southern Africa at Cape Town, as a fueling station for ships on the journey to Asia. Even in an age of colonial abuses of native peoples, the company was a byword for brutality in its treatment of its local workers. It was also highly lucrative for its shareholders. From 1602 to 1696 it paid annual dividends of never less than 12 percent and sometimes as high as 63 percent.

The focus moves north

The prominence in maritime trade of the Dutch, British, and French coincided with the gradual decline in the importance in the European economy of gold and silver from the New World. The economic focus of Europe shifted away from Spain, Italy, and the Mediterranean toward the north. In 1609 the first exchange bank opened in Amsterdam in the Netherlands. This public bank allowed people to make deposits, exchange currency, and later, take out loans. The bank provided a safe home for its depositors' money and used the gold and silver it thus acquired as a guarantee to offer credit, actively promoting trade and industry. Later in the 17th century the first public banks—underwritten by government money—were established in Sweden and England, the Riksbank (1656) and the Bank of England (1694) respectively.

Such banks, like modern banks, operated what is known as a fractional-reserve banking system. In such a system a bank issues notes that are redeemable against its physical holdings of gold, but the total value of the notes issued is greater than the actual value of the gold deposits. In other words, the bank's liabilities exceed its reserves. Such a practice is possible because not all a bank's creditors will ever want to withdraw their deposits at the same time.

Paper money, which had been used in China for centuries, emerged in the West in the 16th century as promissory bills issued by banks against their deposits. Bills proliferated in numerous forms: French colonial authorities in Canada used playing cards signed by the governor as a promise of payment from 1685, since shipment of money from France was slow. Paper money became common in Europe from the 18th century, but remained credit money, meaning that it could be redeemed against deposits of gold or silver.

Economic downturn

In the second half of the 17th century falling shipments of bullion from the New World and the end of the Thirty Years' War brought a downturn in economic activity in Europe. Most European states reacted by adopting protectionist trade systems for the benefit of merchant capitalists, imposing taxes on imports in order to protect domestic business.

During this period of general contraction the Dutch Republic dominated the European economy. Not only did the Dutch control the lucrative Asian spice trade. Thanks to their maritime dominance, in particular the development of the deep-hulled flyboat, the Dutch also controlled the rich trades in North Sea herring and Newfoundland cod, and dominated much of the trade in the Baltic Sea. Dutch seafaring expertise was matched by the development of the insurance business. The chief port, Amsterdam, also became an economic powerhouse: a marketplace, a world bank, and an insurance center. The Dutch Republic's main rivals, England and France, could only work against its commercial supremacy, which they overthrew in the 18th century.

SEE ALSO:

• Volume 2, page 48: Finance and accounting

• Volume 3, page 79: Taxes

• Volume 4, page 35: International trade and finance

• Volume 5, page 49: Inflation and deflation

• Volume 5, page 66: Mercantilism

• Volume 5, page 74: Monopoly

BELOW: Drying cod in early Virginia. In the 17th century Europeans exploited their overseas territories for rich supplies of natural resources.

The Age of Reason and early industrialization

Like many other fields of thinking, economics—called political economy—flourished in the 18th century, when Europeans set out on a systematic examination of the world in which they lived. Agricultural and technological advances, however, were set to change that world forever.

ABOVE: Barely imaginable at the start of the 18th century, industrialization made scenes such as this night view of England's Coalbrookdale increasingly common by century's end.

The late 17th and 18th century marked the birth of modern economics and the formulation of many economic theories that remain highly influential. In the so-called Age of Reason many Europeans became confident that by studying things in an objective, scientific way, humankind could come to understand virtually everything about the workings of the natural and human worlds. Thinkers undertook some of the earliest systematic studies of economic life, which they often related to other fields, particularly politics and demographics. Among the most significant results of the rise of "political economy" as an academic discipline was that the previously dominant doctrine of mercantilism was challenged by arguments for free trade, unrestricted by regulations, taxes, or import tariffs.

Government and trade

At the start of the 18th century it seemed to many Europeans that the overseas expansion of the previous centuries was set to continue. The great joint-stock ventures—led by the English and Dutch East India Companies—had come to dominate the economies and the government of large colonial empires. Their consistent profits encouraged the establish-

Speculation and failure

ABOVE: *The collapse of the South Sea Company did not end British interest in challenging Spanish dominance in the waters around South America. This engraving from 1744 shows the triumphant return to London of Admiral George Anson after attacking Spanish commerce in the region.*

The early 18th century was a time of intense popular speculation in overseas ventures by companies that promised their stockholders rich returns on their investments. As speculation boomed, however, investors backed increasingly ambitious or risky ventures. Around 1720 the collapse of two great companies in Britain and France brought an abrupt end to popular enthusiasm for joint-stock companies.

The South Sea Company was an English firm, founded in 1711 to carry out slave trading in Spanish America. Paying a guaranteed 6 percent dividend a year, the company's stock sold well. Investors were also optimistic—mistakenly, as it turned out—that the War of the Spanish Succession (1701–1714) would end with a treaty allowing increased business in the region. Although the company's first trading voyage in 1717 was only moderately successful, the appointment of King George I as governor of the company boosted investors' confidence.

In 1720 the value of the company's stock increased tenfold in six months when, with the support of the government, the company proposed to take over Britain's national debt. Investors rushed to buy South Sea stock: those who failed were often swindled into making "similar" investments elsewhere. In

September, however, what became known as the South Sea Bubble burst. The market collapsed, and by the year's end company shares had fallen below their level before the boom. Many investors were ruined.

The South Sea Bubble was not the only occasion when speculators had lost out. The collapse of the Mississippi Scheme in 1720 devastated French and European investors. There had been a foretaste of such events in the first half of the 17th century, when ordinary Dutch families had mortgaged their homes or businesses to buy tulip bulbs. At the height of the so-called tulip mania, from 1633 to 1637, the price of rare bulbs rose astronomically. A factory or a house might be exchanged for a single bulb. In 1637, however, a sudden loss of confidence saw the market collapse, leaving many investors ruined.

Such spectacular business collapses were an extreme manifestation of the business cycle, which may have booms and busts. Rapid growth gives way to rapid contraction. Similar events occurred in the stock market crashes of 1887 and 1929, both of which led to international depression. It is an economic priority of most modern governments to find a way to achieve sustained growth that is not so rapid that it invites collapse.

ment of new companies to undertake overseas ventures. Such companies found it relatively easy to raise large amounts of business capital by pooling the resources of numerous investors seeking high returns.

Enthusiasm for joint-stock ventures had a downside, however. Overoptimism on the part of investors and, often, unscrupulous dealing on the part of the companies themselves encouraged excessive speculation in overseas ventures. Most of the investors came from Europe's rich or moderately wealthy citizens. Eventually, some of the most ambitious enterprises collapsed, notably the South Sea Company in England (*see* box, page 39) and the Mississippi Scheme, an ill-fated French plan to sponsor settlement in North America.

Such financial disasters had effects far beyond the ruination of their investors. In England the Parliament severely curtailed the use of corporate organization in business for more than a century after

1720. More generally, the mid–18th century saw more commentators begin to criticize the close link between business ventures and government. In France, in particular, a school of thought emerged that advocated the free play of economic activity. This group, known as the physiocrats, introduced the term *laissez-faire* to economics; literally, the French term means "let it do."

The physiocrats

The physiocrats were opposed to interventionist practices by which governments used laws and taxes to influence the economy. They were also committed to preserving the importance of landowners over merchant capitalists. According to the physiocrats, all wealth originated in agriculture rather than in trade or industry. Regulations on behalf of merchants—such as grants of monopoly and other interventions by the state—contravened what the theorists regarded as a natural law of economic behavior. This law asserted that private property, freedom of trade, and national defense provided the structure within which economic activity should be allowed to take its own course, the doctrine that came to be known as laissez-faire.

One of the leading physiocrats, François Quesnay (1694–1774), was the first person to construct an input-output model of the economy. In his emphasis on large-scale, general factors, Quesnay anticipated the field now known as macroeconomics. Quesnay's diagrammatic representation of the flow of payments and goods among the economic sectors of society was a forerunner of modern input-output analysis, developed in the 20th century by Wassily Leontief (*see* page 99).

The physiocrats believed that economic life had a natural order and that any interference in it by the state would be harmful. Reacting against the conventional economic doctrines of their time, which were rooted in mercantilist principles by which governments shaped economies in order to accumulate national wealth, the physiocrats were harbingers of the free-market system. According to them the state's only proper economic role was to protect property and uphold the natural order.

Physiocracy and Enlightenment

The physiocrats were notable figures in the 18th-century intellectual movement known as the Enlightenment. This movement, which was particularly influential in France, advocated the dominance of reason over emotion and conscience over regulation. In some ways the physiocrats' advocacy of commercial freedom reflected pleas for liberty in matters of conscience made by French philosophers such as

BELOW: Scottish financier John Law was the architect of the ill-fated Mississippi scheme, which led to a stock-market crash and a loss of confidence in joint-stock ventures throughout Europe.

Voltaire, the pen-name of François-Marie Arouet, and Jean-Jacques Rousseau. Rousseau argued for the need for everyone to achieve personal fulfillment and placed a new emphasis on the satisfaction of emotional needs.

Faith in the power of reason led to a parallel emphasis on the importance of disseminating knowledge. Like other leading figures of the Enlightenment, Quesnay contributed articles to the *Encyclopédie*, edited by Denis Diderot. This vast undertaking aimed to provide a digest of current knowledge and theories in many useful fields of endeavor.

The primacy of agriculture

Physiocrats believed that the productive class of the economy comprised people engaged in agriculture and the production of primary goods. Farmers accumulated the wealth that, through trade, was distributed to other groups in society. Commerce and industry were essentially nonproductive: agriculture alone could increase national wealth.

Physiocrats maintained that the revenue of the state should be raised by a single direct tax levied on the land. Only the agricultural classes were capable of producing a surplus, or net product, from which the state could find the capital to expand the flow of goods or levy taxes. Other activities, such as manufacturing, were sterile because they did not produce new wealth but transformed or circulated the output of the productive class. If industry did not create wealth, then, the physiocrats claimed, it was futile for the state to try to enhance society's wealth by detailed regulation and direction of economic activity.

ABOVE: *One of the major figures of the Enlightenment, Jean-Jacques Rousseau advocated a form of personal fulfillment that would later seem to conflict with life in industrialized societies.*

LEFT: *Denis Diderot and his colleagues, possibly including François Quesnay, discuss the progress of Diderot's vast* Encyclopédie. *The 28-volume undertaking, which took 20 years' work, provided a comprehensive and influential survey of Enlightenment thinking on many practical subjects, including economics.*

Adam Smith and *The Wealth of Nations*

Universally regarded as the founding father of modern economics, Adam Smith was born in 1723 at Kirkcaldy, a small town near Edinburgh in Scotland. He studied at the universities of Glasgow and Oxford before returning to Glasgow at the age of 28 to take up a post as professor of logic. It was Smith who formulated the influential notion that the competitive market acts like an "invisible hand" on the economy. Individuals make choices and decisions based on self-interest, and the market itself—rather than regulation or artificial restrictions—will ensure that resources are allocated to the benefit of all.

Smith began delivering public lectures in Edinburgh during his mid-20s, and it was there that he first spoke of the economic philosophy of "the obvious and simple system of natural liberty." It was also during this time that he met the influential philosopher and economist David Hume, who became a close friend.

After 13 years Smith left Glasgow to become tutor to the young duke of Buccleuch. On leaving this post in 1766, he was given a pension of £300 per year by the duke; at a time when the average salary was around £30 per year, this amounted to a considerable income. The pension allowed Smith to spend the next 10 years working in Kirkcaldy and London on *An Inquiry into the Nature and Causes of the Wealth of Nations*, which was eventually published in 1776. This book was the first major work of laissez-faire or free-market economics. It put forward the theory that the best possible economic and social outcome will arise from an economic system based on the self-interest of individuals, rather than from a system based on external intervention and control, such as regulations imposed by a government. According to Smith, each participant in a competitive market is "led by an invisible hand to promote an end which was no part of his intention." Smith's theory became the cornerstone of classical economics in the western world and remains at the heart of most economic thinking today.

Smith and the classical economics he initiated assume that everyone within the market is motivated purely by self-interest. Consumers are motivated by the desire to maximize the satisfaction they get from consuming a good or using a service, be it eating a sandwich or seeing their favorite singer give a concert. Producers, meanwhile, want to maximize the profit they get from selling those sandwiches or from putting on that concert or show. Workers, renters, and capitalists also want to maximize the money they receive from the factors—labor, natural resources, capital—that they own. Such people seek to maximize the wages they get for making sandwiches or from rigging the lights in the concert arena. They want to maximize the rent they can get for leasing the property where the sandwich shop is based, from hiring out the concert hall or PA system for the concert, and so on.

Adam Smith argued that this economic system was not as chaotic as it might seem. The thousands and thousands of separate transactions between different people would actually allocate resources efficiently to the best possible benefit of all those involved and thus to the best possible benefit of society as a whole. There was no need for the government or for any other body to intervene to direct resources; the "invisible hand" would do the job. The work also explained how specialization, exchange, and the development of money could lead to a massive increase in the production of goods and services.

While Smith was writing *The Wealth of Nations*, Britain was going through the early stages of what became known as the Industrial Revolution. New technologies in agriculture, transportation, and manufacturing revolutionized the economy. Many people felt that the growing British market needed to be protected from cheap imports so that the country could build up its reserves of gold to finance further industrialization. As a result, the economic system was based on protectionism, economic restrictions, and legal constraints on trade. Smith's advocacy of "free trade" thus went against conventional economic thought.

After the publication of his book in 1776 Smith was appointed commissioner of customs and of salt duties, and went to live in Edinburgh with his mother. He remained there until his death on July 17, 1790, at the age of 67. Smith seems to have been planning two major treatises—one on the theory and history of law, and one on the sciences and arts—but shortly before his death he had most of his manuscripts destroyed. He had apparently devoted a large part of his considerable income to many secret acts of charity during his life.

ABOVE: *This Scottish penny commemorates Adam Smith by showing some symbols of free trade on a quayside; the other side has Smith's portrait.*

Absolutism

The economic theories of late 17th- and 18th-century Europe evolved in a world dominated by absolutism. Advocates of absolutism believed that complete obedience to a single will was the only way to achieve order in a state, which would be strengthened by having a strong individual at its head. Strong government resulted from the exercise of power by a single ruler, usually a monarch, unrestrained by the church, the nobility, or elected political bodies. The most influential example of such a monarch was Louis XIV, who ruled France from 1643 to 1715. Louis asserted, "L'état, c'est moi," or "I am the state," identifying himself with the nation-state. In the 17th and 18th centuries absolutist monarchs ruled Spain, Prussia, Austria, and Russia.

Absolutist economic policy was far removed from laissez-faire principles. Louis XIV's finance minister, Jean-Baptiste Colbert, revised the system of tariffs on imports, for example, and encouraged the development of industry and new companies. Increased industrial output, he believed, would bring France an increased share of international trade, which would be carried in the high-quality merchant fleet he had built. Such moves ultimately failed in the face of foreign tariffs—the Dutch and the French went to war over tariffs in 1672–1678—and the resentment by French traders of government intervention in their business.

With hindsight, Colbert's system had a negative effect on the French economy. Far from encouraging growth, the subjugation of business to the state and the proliferation of bureaucracy to control it left the economy stagnant and inefficient in the 18th century as other states, such as Britain, began to modernize.

ABOVE: *Louis XIV, the "Sun King," dressed here to play the Sun in a ballet, set the example for Europe's absolute rulers. Grandeur and display made an important contribution to a ruler's personal and political prestige.*

Classical economics

Physiocracy contained many innovative ideas, but in some ways it appeared outdated almost as soon as it appeared. Its central tenet—that agriculture took precedence over other economic activity—was at odds with the growing importance of manufacturing. Technological development, although it was ignored by the physiocrats, was stimulating a process of industrialization in parts of Europe that proved to be the beginning of the period that is often called the Industrial Revolution. When the influential Scottish economist Adam Smith (1724–1796) met the French theorists in Paris in the 1760s, he was impressed by their antimercantilist ideas but also realized that their "natural law" had serious inherent shortcomings as an economic theory.

The Wealth of Nations

The foundation of classical economics, *The Wealth of Nations*, by Adam Smith (see box), is the most important and influential book on the subject ever published. It incorporated some of the physiocrats' ideas with theories Smith had developed earlier in his career. When the book first appeared, in 1776, the concept of free trade was already finding a following in both Britain and America. Although the book received an enthusiastic reception in some quarters, not everybody was immediately convinced of Smith's cause. The British government, for example, remained mercantilist in outlook for many decades to come.

As its title implies, *The Wealth of Nations* is an analysis of the factors that increase the financial power of a community or state. Smith rejected what he called the "false doctrines of political economy" advocated by mercantilist theories, which emphasized the accumulation of gold and silver as the path to national wealth. Instead, Smith examined some of the ways in which a free enterprise system might achieve greater prosperity.

Surveying the world economy, Smith discovered an enormous mass of what he saw as useless or harmful regulations. He concluded that it was desirable to do away with such restraints on business and give free play to the economic forces of supply and demand. He believed that "all systems either of restraint or preference being thus completely taken away, the obvious and simple system of natural liberty establishes itself of its own accord."

Self-interest

Smith's system stressed the importance of permitting individuals to follow their self-interest as a means of promoting national prosperity. Self-interest, he believed, was not only the motivating force of all economic activity, but also the source of the greatest public good. "It is not from the benevolence of the butcher, the brewer or the baker that we expect our dinner," he wrote, "but from their regard to their own interest. We address ourselves not to their humanity but to their self-love." In other words, people worked in order to make money or support themselves, not because of a charitable impulse to help others.

Self-interest motivated individual transactions, Smith argued. Prices were determined by the totality of all transactions put together, in what Smith dubbed the "invisible hand" of the market. The market ensured that innumerable self-interested activities by individuals resulted in the best outcome for the whole of society, or optimum production. Thus Smith argued against the traditional hostility to self-enrichment, which dated back at least to the ancient Greek philosopher Aristotle. On the contrary, Smith argued, individual economic ambition was a necessary contribution to the public good.

The price of commodities might be decided by supply and demand in the market, but labor, not mercantilist gold and silver, was the basic measure of economic wealth. By bringing prices into the economic equation, Smith gave economics its modern structure and established the principles of value and distribution. It was Smith who first proposed what has become known as the Labor Theory of Value, according to which price is determined by the quantity of labor involved in production and the cost of sustaining it. A nation's wealth, Smith believed, was enhanced first by "the skill, dexterity and judgment with which its labor is applied; and, secondly, by the proportion between the number of those who are employed in useful labor, and that of those who are not so employed."

The division of labor

In *The Wealth of Nations* Adam Smith described specialization by individuals, which he called the division of labor. Smith used as an example the manufacture of pins. In a famous example he described how a pinmaker carrying out all stages of the process might make 20 pins a day. Smith proposed a process by which the production of each pin was divided into a number of different stages. One worker drew out the wire, another straightened it, a third cut it, a fourth pointed, a fifth ground it at the top for fitting the pinhead, and so on. In such a way, Smith argued,

ABOVE: *A contemporary portrait of David Ricardo.*

10 workers specializing in each stage of the process could make 48,000 pins a day.

Smith also argued that it was only possible for someone to specialize in making pins all day if he or she knew that they would be able to exchange their labor for other goods and services such as food, housing, and transport. In other words, specialization of labor would increase the importance of exchange and the importance of mechanisms to allow exchange, such as money, for example. Specialization also led to interdependence among members of an economy.

The price of labor

Smith saw capital as necessary to secure a plant and machinery, and also to cover the cost of bringing the worker into production and keeping him or her there. Smith referred to "the price of labor," as if labor were just another commodity. In fact, his approach to labor was more humane than that of some of the later economists who developed his ideas. In opposition to conventional wisdom, Smith insisted on the "economy of high wages," meaning that well-paid workers were likely to work better than poorer paid ones. In his survey of political economy he gave the highest priority to the provision of plentiful income for the masses of the people. The most decisive test of the prosperity of a nation is the growth of the population: as the number of people grows, the increase in numbers brings an increase in general prosperity.

Smith also described the importance of competition in capitalist societies as the stimulus toward optimal industrial efficiency. He recognized, however, that businesses sometimes believed that they could benefit more without competition. "People of the same trade," he complained, "seldom meet together, even for merriment and diversion, but the meeting ends in a conspiracy against the public, or in some contrivance to raise prices."

David Ricardo

The man who developed Smith's economic theories, the Englishman David Ricardo (1772–1823), made a fortune on the Stock Exchange and was able to retire at the age of 42. Great weight was attached to his opinions on economic questions, and he exerted immense political influence. His early publications were on money and banking, but in *The Principles of Political Economy and Taxation* (1817) he produced a work that dominated classical economics for more than 50 years.

Ricardo's book sought to "determine the laws which regulate the distribution (between the different classes of landowners, capitalists, and labor) of the produce of industry." Ricardo believed that the allocation of output and resources among the various social classes was determined by the economic bases of individualism, competition, self-interest, and private property. This was similar to Adam Smith's idea of an "invisible hand."

Basing his work on the complexities of an actual economy, Ricardo abstracted principles to construct a theoretical model that would reveal the fundamental influences at work in economic life. Ricardo invented the concept of the "economic model"—a logical apparatus consisting of a few variables that could predict, after some manipulation, results of practical significance. Economists still use models to explain economic actions and to make predictions by the theoretical simplification of more complex economic realities.

An agricultural model

Ricardo's economic model was predominantly agricultural. Influenced by the population studies of his friend Thomas Malthus (*see* box), he argued that a constantly growing population would force up demand for land, causing less fertile land to be brought into cultivation. Yields would steadily diminish

Thomas Malthus

In 1798 Thomas Malthus published *An Essay on the Principle of Population as it affects the Future Improvement of Society*, whose ideas on population growth had a profound impact on contemporary economic and political thinking. Malthus's pessimistic theory of economics argued that population growth would outstrip the growth of food supplies, thus undermining any chance for continuing prosperity. Population, Malthus argued, tended to double exponentially with each generation, from 2 to 4 to 8 to 16 and so on. Food, on the other hand, would increase in an arithmetical progression, from 2 to 4 to 6 to 8 and so on.

The doubling of the population could be checked either by nature or by human prudence. According to Malthus, "the power of population is so superior to the power of the earth to produce subsistence for man, that premature death must in some shape or other visit the human race." Those shapes included war, disease, and famine, which combined to bring the world's population down to the point at which the food supply could sustain it.

The only escape from population pressure that avoided such horrors, Malthus argued, was by the voluntary limitation of population. As a Catholic, Malthus rejected the use of contraception to limit the birthrate. Instead, he argued that the same end could be realized by late marriages, which would consequently lead to smaller families. Thus Malthus came to be seen as a gloomy advocate of moral restraint; his ideas earned economics its popular name as "the dismal science."

ABOVE: Thomas Malthus has a reputation as a somewhat gloomy moralist for his pessimistic view of the future and his advocacy of moral restraint.

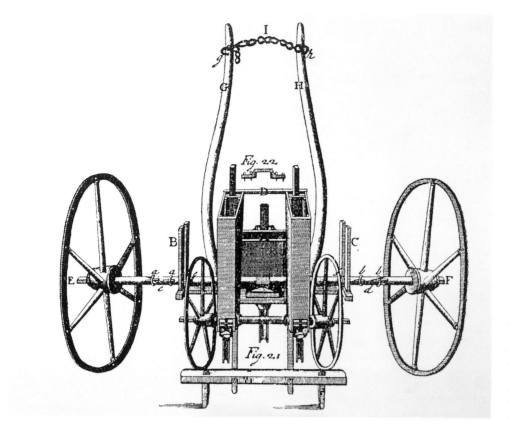

LEFT: The horse-drawn seed drill invented by Jethro Tull allowed the planting of seeds in straight rows that were easier to tend and harvest and thus more economical than grain that had been scattered by hand.

after "a certain and not very advanced stage in the progress of agriculture." The output—of grain or other crops—produced by each additional unit of labor and capital would be less on less fertile land. Labor always cost the same, so more marginal land was relatively more expensive to work. Better profits would attract people to invest in nonmarginal land until the law of diminishing returns caused those profits to fall in line with the profits on the marginal land. Because costs and profits were the same in both cases, a surplus was earned on the fertile, nonmarginal land. Ricardo defined this surplus as rent.

The law of comparative costs
Ricardo anticipated that economic growth would eventually fail, owing to the rising cost of growing food in a limited area. One solution to a shortage of grain would be to import cheap wheat from abroad. Ricardo believed that England would benefit from specializing in manufacturing goods and exporting them in return for food. To support his case, he formulated the "law of comparative costs."

Ricardo assumed that labor and capital move freely within countries to seek the highest returns, but could not do so as easily between countries. In these circumstances, he showed, the benefits of trade are determined by a comparison of costs within each country, rather than a comparison between countries. It pays a country to specialize in the production of goods that it can produce more efficiently, or relatively cheaply, and to exchange such goods for imports of all other goods.

A country such as Portugal, for example, might be able to produce all goods more cheaply, than, say, Britain. It would nevertheless be well advised to concentrate its resources on wine production, in which its efficiency is greater than in its other manufacturing, and to import British textiles. Ricardo's argument asserted that if all countries took full advantage of the "territorial division of labor," total world output would be larger than if countries tried to become self-sufficient. Ricardo's law became the basis of the 19th-century doctrine of free trade.

Ricardo's influence
Ricardo's treatise had an immediate impact, and the Ricardian system dominated economic thinking in Britain for half a century. In 1848 the restatement of Ricardian thought in John Stuart Mill's *Principles of Political Economy* gave it renewed authority (*see* page 56). Ricardo's subsequent influence can be seen in the stress laid by some economists on capital and in their neglect of Adam Smith's more humanitarian ideas about labor.

Ricardo's principles are often interpreted to mean that the working classes were somehow "meant" to be poor and that their conditions should not be relieved by the state, employers, or trades unions. Workers' low income was the result of the equilibrium price of labor, the level at which wages settled when the quantity of labor needed matched the quantity available. Ricardo saw wages not as a means for workers to better themselves, but solely as "that price which is necessary to enable the laborers to subsist and perpetuate their race, without increase or diminution." Ricardo also believed, however, that investment and the development of technology would lead to an indefinite rise in wages in any particular industry.

The Agrarian Revolution

The changes that occurred in European agriculture between about 1760 and 1830, particularly in Britain, were so momentous that they are sometimes referred to as the Agrarian Revolution. Such developments supported and stimulated developments in industrialization and urbanization and were crucial to support the rising populations needed to supply the industrialized labor force.

Agricultural output in England roughly doubled between 1750 and 1850, while the production of wheat increased fourfold. This increase came mainly through an increase in the land available for cultivation, and to a lesser extent because of changing farm practices. These changes included enclosure and land redistribution (*see* box, page 49), mechanization, new forms of crop rotation (*see* box), selective breeding of livestock, and the invention of the seed drill by Jethro Tull (1674–1741), which made it easier and quick-

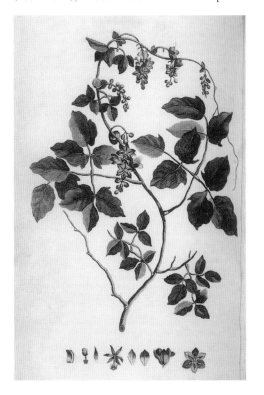

Crop rotation

From early in agricultural history farmers have realized that growing crops exhausts nutrients in soil. The answer, they discovered, was to leave fields to lie fallow and replenish themselves for a season. At its simplest this crop rotation involved leaving half the land empty and growing crops on the rest, then swapping the fields around the following year. Such a procedure had the disadvantage of meaning that half the land was unproductive in any year. In medieval Europe, therefore, villages and estates had adopted a three-field system (*see* page 18). In this system only a third of the land lies fallow in each year, the other two-thirds being used to produce a spring crop and a fall crop respectively.

The Agrarian Revolution brought developments that made it no longer necessary to leave fields fallow every third year. One of the major innovations that enabled this was the introduction of new fodder crops, especially turnips and legumes. Farmers discovered that such crops helped replenish nitrates and nutrients in depleted soil. Animals fed on the crops produced a better quality of manure to spread on the land, further encouraging the replenishment of the soil.

---

er to plant seeds. Other important factors included the application of artificial fertilizers and improved clay soils. The increased use of horses to draw plows allowed soil to be heavily tilled, while increased grain production was secured by various Corn Laws that governed the import and export of grain.

The high productivity of British agriculture contrasted with the comparatively low output on mainland Europe, enabling the British Isles to support a rapidly expanding nonagricultural population. As demand for food and thus prices rose, a rise in agricultural incomes also fueled demand for domestic manufactured goods and services, and helped transfer capital from the land to industry.

New breeds

By the late 18th century the output per acre on British farms was higher than that of any other European country. Agricultural production supplied the raw materials for industry and produced fodder for the thousands of horses used in manufacturing, farming, mining, and transport. The greater use of animal rather than human power was itself one of the most important innovations that enabled the productivity of British farms to outstrip that of farms in continental Europe.

LEFT: Widely practiced in Europe's American colonies, cotton growing benefited immensely from the introduction of the cotton gin, invented by Eli Whitney in 1793.

LEFT: *This illustration from Denis Diderot's* Encyclopédie *shows contemporary agricultural technology in action, including, in the foreground, a seed drill and a new type of horse-drawn plow.*

Scientific developments to improve animal stocks by selective breeding began in the early 18th century. New breeding techniques met a demand for meat fueled by urbanization and an ever-improving transportation system. Seed drills and horse-drawn hoes came into operation during the late 17th century but were not widely used until later, when Jethro Tull's improvements made it far easier for people to plant crops. In 1786 Andrew Meikle built a threshing machine that could do in a day what had taken a group of laborers five days. Because of the large pool of cheap labor available in the countryside, however, the introduction of tools and machinery happened only slowly. It was only during times of labor shortage, such as those experienced in the Napoleonic Wars (1800–1815), that investment in machinery really made an impact.

Feeding Britain's rapidly expanding population required an efficient transportation system to distribute produce. Accompanying this change were more regularized rules governing weights and measures to assist large-scale dealing. As a result, the supply of grain, meat, fruit, and vegetables to towns greatly improved. Road and canal building, coastal shipping, and the later creation of the railroad network were also significant factors behind agricultural distribution and development.

Enclosure and its consequences

The Agrarian Revolution changed the agricultural landscape of Britain. Enclosure, or the partitioning of open land by fences or hedges, had been occurring since the medieval period; but in the 1760s and 1770s, and again during the Napoleonic Wars at the start of the 19th century, Britain experienced an upturn in land reclamation and enclosure. The reclamation of waste and marginal land permitted the growth of larger farms. Large landowners also bene-

Enclosure

Enclosure, or the gradual consolidation of communally owned arable fields into carefully delineated, privately owned plots, had begun in Europe in the 12th century. Previously, most farmland had comprised huge fields divided into strips that were worked by individual cultivators or families between sowing time and harvest. In the winter the fields had reverted to common land that local people used for grazing livestock. Enclosed land was surrounded by fences or hedges, thus preventing the exercise of such traditional rights.

In England most enclosure occurred between 1750 and 1860. By the end of the 19th century virtually all England's common lands had gone. In the rest of Europe the process occurred rather later. In Denmark, France, and Germany it came in the mid-19th century; in Russia the process began after the emancipation of the serfs in 1861. In Poland and Czechoslovakia, on the other hand, enclosure did not take place until after the end of World War I in 1918.

fited from the enclosure of common lands (*see* box). Many smallholders relied for subsistence on their ancient rights to use common lands to graze their animals or gather firewood. Enclosure left them unable to feed their families, and many were forced to sell to large landowners. Enclosure also gave landlords a chance to raise rents during the necessary renegotiation of leases.

The loss of common lands created a population of underemployed female and young workers. Such people were drawn into industrial employment or into the service sector in the urban centers. Some failed to find any employment. The late 18th-century labor market was characterized by a growth of unemployment, particularly among those who had worked on small farms.

The Steam Age

The process of industrialization in Great Britain in the second half of the 18th century profoundly altered the country's economy and society. The most immediate changes came in production and affected what was produced, as well as where and how. Labor was trans-

ABOVE: A coalminer makes his way home in this British print from the early 19th century. Behind him an early steam locomotive pulls a load of coal away from the colliery.

ferred from the provision of primary products, such as coal and iron, to the production of consumer goods and services. More manufactured goods were produced than ever before, and technical efficiency increased dramatically. In part, the growth in productivity was achieved by the systematic application of scientific and practical knowledge to manufacturing processes, with streamlined procedures and innovative technology. Efficiency was also enhanced when numbers of similar or interdependent enterprises grew up in limited areas. Specialization and interdependence became increasingly important. A town that had a number of cotton mills, for example, would attract related operations such as dyeing works. These concentrations of industry became the centers of urbanization as increasing numbers of people migrated from the countryside to the towns.

Social upheaval

One of the consequences of the switch from agrarian, rural-based occupations to urban industries and services was a rapid increase in employment. This transformation was accompanied by sometimes violent social unrest, however. The new jobs were perceived as a

ABOVE: A woman operates a spinning jenny. Invented by James Hargreaves in 1764, the machine enabled a single worker to spin eight bobbins of cotton at once, rather than one. A later version could spin 16 bobbins.

threat to traditional, skilled jobs. Workers anxious to protect their livelihoods rioted and broke new machines. Political campaigners meanwhile protested to regulate the conditions in factories and mills, where adults and children worked long hours with minimal comforts, often in danger from machinery that had no safety guards. New laws tackled the problem of the poor and unemployed, creating workhouses where the destitute could be supported, albeit at a minimal level.

Growing workforce

The release of capital and labor from the land to the industrial sector was earlier and faster in Britain than in any other country in Europe. The growing urban labor force created an enlarged domestic demand for goods and services, which in turn sustained the rapid population growth and urbanization.

Significant changes occurred in the way in which work was organized. People worked increasingly for firms in factories, rather than in the home or manor-based workshops. Industrial production became heavily dependent on the intensive use of equipment to increase efficiency. New tools and machinery, particularly in industries such as textile production, allowed workers to produce more goods by specializing in one particular part of the process. Jobs generally became more mundane for workers who had to operate one machine that repeated a simple task countless times. For many people such jobs were unrewarding and robbed them of any sense of pride they might have taken in producing something from start to finish.

Mechanical power

The fundamental characteristic of industrialization was the introduction of mechanical power to replace human and animal power in the production of goods and services.

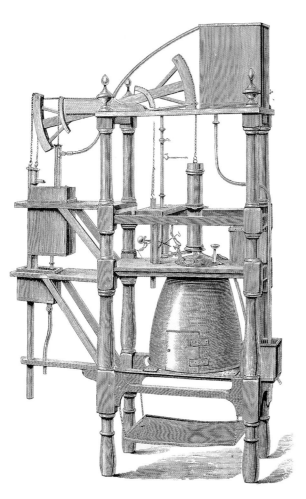

LEFT: The original model of Thomas Newcomen's steam engine, invented in 1707. The engine, which converted the energy of steam into mechanical energy, was the basis of much later mechanization.

Numerous technological developments benefited British manufacturing. Thomas Newcomen had patented a steam-driven pumping engine in 1707; in 1769 James Watt dramatically improved the design, allowing pumps to be used to drain mines. In 1801 Richard Trevithick first used a steam engine to power a moving vehicle. In 1733 John Kay invented the flying shuttle for weavers, while James Hargreaves developed the spinning jenny in 1764. Five years later Richard Arkwright patented a spinning machine that he combined in his mills with systematic industrial organization. Edmund Cartwright patented the first power loom in 1786. Meanwhile, the work of Abraham Darby and his descendants at Coalbrookdale in Shropshire typified the developing British mastery of cast-iron manufacture. The world's first cast-iron structure, built from 1777 to 1779, gave the name Ironbridge to the town where it still stands.

The reasons for success

Britain's economy thrived for a number of different reasons. One was the emergence of private commercial enterprises—banks and insurance companies, for example—that stimulated the development of paper substitutes for coins in the form of banknotes, bills of exchange, book credit, and checks. Such developments ensured the supply of the nation's money at a time when gold and silver bullion was often exported and coins melted down to extract their valuable minerals. Paper money and credit laid the foundations of a modern financial system.

Another cause of success was technological innovation. The emphasis on trade helped focus inventors' minds on manufacture, particularly on the production of textiles and the making of iron and steel. The factory system, meanwhile, drew on an established culture of home or manor-based manufactures, easing the transition from a protoindustrial to an industrial society.

Industrialization spreads

The process of industrialization experienced in Britain was the forerunner of later developments in many of the countries of western Europe and in the United States. France, Belgium, and what is now Germany led the way in the industrialization of continental Europe, concentrating first on primary industries such as coal and iron production and then increasingly on manufacturing. The United States followed the same general pattern. All the countries affected by industrial-

ABOVE: This 19th-century view of Ironbridge shows the world's first cast-iron structure, the bridge, built by Abraham Darby in the 1770s.

AMSTELDAM

ization underwent an accompanying process of urbanization and suffered to a greater or lesser degree the social problems experienced in Britain.

Colonial economies

One of the chief elements in most of Europe's major economies in the late 18th century and early 19th centuries was trade with overseas colonies. By the beginning of the 19th century most Spanish, Portuguese, and French colonies in the Americas had become independent. The Dutch, however, had established a settlement at the Cape of Good Hope to support sea voyages to Asia and by 1800 controlled Java and Ceylon (now Sri Lanka). Britain also remained an important colonial power, despite having lost most of its North American colonies except Canada after the American Revolutionary War (1773–1783). The British East India Company had begun the conquest of the Indian subcontinent in 1757.

In mercantilist theory the purpose of colonies was to provide their parent countries with precious metals and the raw materials on which export industries depended. Once established, therefore, colonial settlements were supposed to trade exclusively with their respective parent nations. Legislation such as Britain's Navigation Act of 1764 tried to reinforce the secondary status of colonies by insisting that exports from British colonies had to be shipped in British vessels to British ports, from where they could be reexported.

Losing North America

Such a process, by stimulating industry in the colonies, encouraged colonial populations to react against mercantile practices. The treatment of colonies as little more than supply depots and their exclusion from trade with other nations damaged their economies. Resentment against such a situation was a key cause of the American Revolutionary War. One of the patriots' main goals was freedom to trade elsewhere, not only with Britain.

Despite the loss of the United States, the British Empire continued to expand and provided expanding foreign markets for British goods. The empire was at once both an economic and a military entity. Trade and the opening and protection of foreign markets became one of the main roles of the British

ABOVE: This print shows Amsterdam in the 18th century. Although Britain's industrial development made it Europe's leading commercial power, the Dutch empire in Southeast Asia remained a source of substantial national wealth.

ABOVE: The human cost of developing trade: in a "barracoon" in Sierra Leone, Africa, slaves await shipment to the Americas. Captives were chained by the neck and legs, and frequently flogged in the months for which they were sometimes held in Africa.

army and navy. The War of Jenkins' Ear in 1739, for example, was triggered by British traders' incursions into the Spanish Empire. Mercantilist theory of the 17th and 18th centuries specifically advocated the use of the state's armed might to defend and promote a nation's economic interests.

The benefits of war

As well as creating and guarding new markets for British goods, military activity created and increased demand for military products and thus stimulated technological innovation generally. The demands of the War of the Austrian Succession (1740–1748) led to pioneering improvements in techniques for smelting coke. The introduction of the flying shuttle for weaving looms coincided with the Seven Years' War (1756–1763), for which numerous new uniforms were required. The major impact of war was a growth in export demand for British goods. The export trade remained unchallenged as long as Britain's navy ruled the seas, protecting its commerce and providing security for capitalists to invest in the long-term future.

Britain's external trade was crucial since its exported goods consisted primarily of home manufactures. Many of these products could be mass-produced to meet overseas demand, including textiles, iron, and metalware. During the Industrial Revolution both imports and exports grew rapidly. Reexports—where raw materials or partly finished goods were brought to Britain, turned into manufactures, and then sold back to their country of origin—increased by a factor of nine. Because of the protectionist policies adopted by European countries to safeguard their devel-

oping industries, British colonies in the South Asia and the Americas were the main market for Britain's output.

The Atlantic economy

Britain's excellent coastal waters provided an ideal platform for it to exploit the Atlantic economy, though the situation changed in the 1780s after the loss of the North American colonies. One of the most important commodities underpinning the dynamic growth of the Atlantic economy was slaves. Shipping captured Africans across the Atlantic became just one leg of a system of elaborate trade routes that linked Europe, Africa, and various parts of the Americas. Africa, for example became the second largest destination for British iron in the mid-18th century and took almost a quarter of British cotton by the 1790s. The most important domain for British trade from the 1830s on was India, which made up for the decline in trade with the West Indies.

The value of trade

Britain's dominance of world trade by 1800 reflected not just its navy's control of the high seas. The country supported its trade with sophisticated forms of commercial organization and heavy investment in canals and roads, dockyards, and mining. Britain's development and its relationship with its overseas possessions was a case study for other industrializing nations. Without international markets, the cotton trade would not have existed, the woollen and iron industries would have been much smaller, and agriculture would have evolved more slowly. The world's first industrial economy had been shaped by the demands of international trade.

Industrialization, urbanization, and modernization

As the 19th century went on, industrialization and urbanization on a massive scale radically changed the face of large parts of the world. Economists sought to explain the processes taking place and to predict ways nations could maximize their share of booming prosperity.

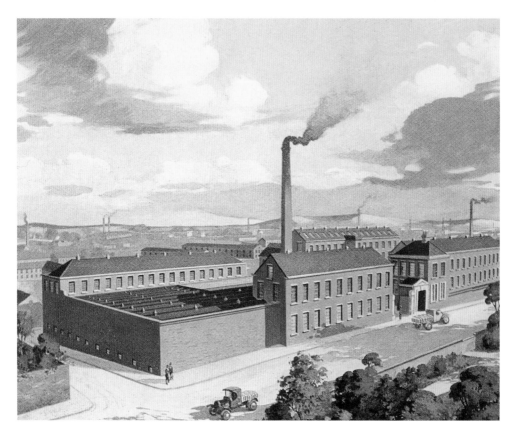

LEFT: Cotton mills, like these in Bolton, Lancashire, became an increasingly common sight in the late 19th century. As in the first half of the century, production became more and more concentrated in large factories surrounded by industrial towns.

Industrialization in the 19th century was driven by the introduction of steam power and the mechanization of labor, when workers started to use machinery to produce goods and services. As mechanized industry gained momentum in England and gradually spread to other parts of the world, production of goods became more specialized and concentrated in larger units, called factories.

The Industrial Revolution

Technology—the systematic application of scientific and practical knowledge—led to a rapid increase in the production of goods and services because it speeded up the manufacturing process. Far more manufactured goods were produced than ever before, and technical efficiency rose dramatically. Tasks became increasingly routine and specialized, while a reliance on tools and machinery allowed individual workers to produce more goods. Specialization meant greater interdependence and as a result increased productivity.

Cotton, the most completely industrialized sector of the British economy, was almost entirely mechanized, steam-powered, and factory-based. Vast new mills contained banks of spinning and weaving machines, operated largely by women and children. The workers gradually gained protection from factory laws restricting working hours and reducing the dangers of handling machinery, despite the resistance to such measures of factory owners.

Europe's industrial development was accompanied by rapid population growth. Improvements in medicine, diet, and living conditions reduced death rates, while urbanization and industrialization saw an increase in birthrates. The population of Europe almost doubled during the century, accelerating the movement from the countryside to the towns. By 1851, for example, half the population of Britain lived in urban areas.

The application of steam power to transportation—first railroads, then steamships—gave another boost to the economy, making it possible to move goods cheaply and in bulk. The railroads also provided a cheap and convenient way for people to move from the countryside to the new industrial towns and increased the concentration of production. They enabled raw materials to be brought from far away and finished goods to be dispatched to distant ports.

Britain's primacy

Although industrialization was spreading throughout Europe and the United States, Britain maintained its industrial primacy. Advances in mechanization and factory production allowed it to supply a large proportion of the world's textiles, iron, and machinery. The adoption of free trade while Robert Peel was prime minister, from 1841 to 1846, stimulated a massive increase in Britain's export income. New industries arose, such as steel and shipbuilding. In the former the Bessemer process—named for British inventor Sir Henry Bessemer—blew air through molten cast iron to produce workable steel. In shipbuilding engineer Isambard Kingdom Brunel (1806–1859) built vast transatlantic steamships such as the *Great Western* (1838) and the *Great Britain* (1843).

In 1851 the Great Exhibition in London was held to show the world Britain's progress in trade and manufacturing. Its economic lead seemed unassailable, but other countries were industrializing fast, with rapid growth in railways, textile industries, and iron and coal production. By the end of the century both the United States and Germany were poised to challenge Britain's dominance.

Free trade and business

The need for machinery and factories for business created a need for large amounts of financial investment. In all the industrial nations laws were changed or enacted to permit the growth of large companies. In this way industrialization provided the impetus for the emergence of the modern corporation, paving the way for the corporate giants that now dominate much of the world economy.

In Britain and elsewhere joint-stock banks with large financial capital bases began to take the place of less reliable local banks. In 1844 Parliament established the role of the Bank of England as the central banknote-issuing authority and guarantor of the rest of the banking system. At about the same time, a series of acts regulated company finance and lending. The growth of trade led to the expansion of the Stock Exchange, and by 1870 London was the world's financial capital.

Despite Britain's economic health, demand for goods within the domestic econ-

BELOW: Traders on the floor of the London Stock Exchange in 1891. During the last quarter of the 19th century, London was the business capital of the world.

omy was often restricted to those with larger incomes and purchasing power. The vast majority could not afford to consume fashionable products. Nevertheless, the expansion of the proletariat—wage earners without capital—did increase the demand for some basic products, such as bread, clothes, and candles.

It was the wealthier members of the growing middle class, however, who provided the market for manufacturers of mass-produced goods. Mechanization made goods abundant and cheap. Consequently, the real standard of living rose throughout much of the world during the 19th century.

Liberal economics

Trade was now firmly associated with noninterference by government in trade and business. Such an attitude reflected the continued dominance of the classical economics estab-

RIGHT: *Economist and politician John Stuart Mill, shown here in a contemporary caricature, restated classical economic theory but linked abstract concepts with a real interest in social concerns.*

lished by Adam Smith in the *Wealth of Nations* (1776) (*see* page 42). Smith's theories and those of his successor, David Ricardo, received an influential restatement in 1848, when John Stuart Mill published *Principles of Political Economy*. Mill's book was an up-to-date version of Adam Smith's work and remained the basic textbook for students of economics until the end of the century.

Classical economists had their arguments during the three-quarters of a century spanning Smith's and Mill's works, but all agreed on certain major principles: the importance of private property, freedom of markets, and in Mill's words, the belief that "only through the principle of competition has political economy any pretension to the character of a science." They shared Smith's strong suspicion of government and his firm confidence in the power of self-interest—that the individual pursuit of private gain would benefit society as a whole. Smith argued that competition would result in the optimal use of labor and capital. During at least the earlier part of the 19th century, when goods were produced in such vast numbers that a highly productive performance was taken for granted, he seemed to have been proved right.

Smith's arguments in favor of free trade were now widely accepted. He asserted that governmental regulation of trade actually reduced the wealth of nations because it prevented them from purchasing the maximum amount of commodities at the lowest possible price. David Ricardo argued that nations could gain from free trade if they concentrated on producing and trading commodities where they had a comparative advantage, meaning that they could produce a good at a relatively cheaper cost in terms of other goods than another nation or producer. This principle has remained the theoretical basis of all arguments for free trade.

British and U.S. industrialization

Despite classical theory, few countries have ever adopted a policy of free trade. Political practicalities have often encouraged governments to adopt at least a partial policy of protection for the domestic economy. The major exception was Britain, which, from the 1840s until the 1930s, levied no import duties of any kind. From the late 1830s, mainly middle-class Britons argued for the repeal of the Corn Laws, which taxed imported grain. When, in 1845–1846, disease destroyed the potato crop in Ireland and widespread famine ensued, the government did repeal the Corn Laws and launched a policy of free trade. Cheaper wheat did not help the starving Irish, however: about 500,000 people died and another million emigrated, mainly to the United States.

In the United States industrialization took a slightly different course. The War of 1812 had given rise to strong feelings of nationalism, and in 1816 Congress was able to increase the high tariff it had levied for the war. This was done to protect the nation's growing manufacturing industries from the great quantities of low-priced imports from Britain.

The northeastern states became a great manufacturing center. Canals and railroads were built between west and east, and powered the growth of the cities of Boston, New York, Philadelphia, and Baltimore because they gave them easier access to the products of the west. The southern states, by contrast, were principally devoted to growing one crop, cotton, on large plantations worked by black slave labor. The cotton flowed unimpeded into British cotton mills. When the Civil War (1861–1865) cut off the supply, the ensuing cotton famine brought great hardship to the mill towns of Britain.

List and the German *Zollverein*

Although economics was primarily a British subject, there were students of economics in other European countries and the United States who saw the issues from a different standpoint. The notions of self-interest, free trade, and market forces encouraged by Adam Smith and his successors implied that the state existed for the individual. German thinkers, in particular, differed significantly from this view,

placing more reliance on the state, which played an important role in the region's move toward full industrialization.

Economists such as Friedrich List (1789–1846) also opposed the classicist's view of economic life as static. They saw it as a development going through successive stages, culminating at maturity with a combination of agricultural, manufacturing, and commercial activity. List believed that the state had an indispensable role in moving everything forward toward this equilibrium.

List had forcefully promoted liberal trading policies between the German states when they formed the free trade customs union, called the *Zollverein*. In 1831, however, when he returned to Germany from a period of exile in the United Sates, he advised adopting tariffs, or entry taxes, for the *Zollverein* as a whole, seeking for the larger region the protection he opposed in its smaller constituent states. List believed that tariffs were essential: a country that had the national and human resources to develop new industries needed to protect them from incoming products.

List's case for protection was taken up in the United States, where it was called the infant-industries argument. The theory argued that although the principle of free trade was sound, there was a valid exception for tariffs that protected and nurtured the development of young and vulnerable industries. In the end, in all of the aspiring industrial countries

LEFT: In despair, Jefferson Davis ponders the evidence of the South's economic ruin in this cartoon from the U.S. Civil War. The cessation of the cotton trade with Britain, along with the damage to the South's infrastructure during the war, subjected the Confederacy to crippling inflation.

U.S. political economy

The population theories of Thomas Malthus (1766–1834) inspired the work of British classical economists such as David Ricardo. Malthus argued that population would grow until it was checked by a lack of food to support its growth, and that food supply could not grow quickly enough to keep up with population growth. If population grows too much relative to food production, it will be halted by famine, disease, and war.

Malthus's theory did not seem very relevant in the United States, however. There, the rapidly expanding population was in possession of a food supply that far from decreasing, was rapidly increasing as new lands were opened up in the west.

America also differed from Europe in other economic matters where Americans perceived the interests of their young country as conflicting with those of the far longer established nations of Europe. With regard to free trade, for example, American statesman Alexander Hamilton (1755–1804) opposed it in cases in which a younger country was in competition with a more established industrializing country, such as Britain. In that case, he argued, the younger country should use protectionist measures to shield its own industries from the free market. Later, the politician Henry Clay (1777–1852) also urged U.S. industrial development under a tariff system known as the American System, in order to reduce U.S. dependence on other nations.

In the South there was little enthusiasm for protectionism. The planters who dominated the southern economy grew raw materials, such as cotton, that were in great demand in Europe. They wanted to export products for manufacture and import inexpensive goods in return. Southern opposition to protectionism threatened to be a serious political force. It was terminated by the Civil War (1861–1865), however, and for the next 70 years the supporters of tariffs would dominate American political economy.

ABOVE: In the late 18th century Alexander Hamilton established the fiscal system of the United States, setting out to stimulate trade and exploit America's vast reserves of natural resources.

tariff protection was in almost all cases granted to new or infant industries. Adam Smith's doctrine was still widely celebrated as truth, but in all countries it yielded to a seemingly special circumstance.

Monopoly and oligopoly

In the late 19th century the tendencies inherent in a free market economy brought new changes in Britain, the United States, and other industrial nations. The modern corporation, with its limited liability and immense financial power, began to emerge as the dominant form of business organization, especially in the United States. This was partly due to technological advances that enabled a handful of large firms to satisfy demand in many markets. It also stemmed from the tactics of the captains of industry, such as the U.S. entrepreneur John D. Rockefeller (1839–1937), who set out to eliminate competitors. In 1879, for example, Rockefeller's Standard Oil lowered kerosene prices to knock out local competition all over the United States and then raised prices to cover its earlier losses.

The result of this kind of activity was not always complete monopoly, in which one company controlled a market, but rather, an economic order known as oligopoly, in which production was dominated by a few firms. Oligopolistic firms sometimes colluded to establish informal agreements that set prices artificially higher than they would have been. Producers wanted it to seem as if competition still existed. One of the means used to achieve this was the trust. The trust was a device by which the control of a company was transferred to an individual or a small group of individuals by exchanging shares in return for trust certificates, which are issued by the individuals seeking control.

Antitrust laws

Such a reduction in competition could not easily be reconciled with classical theory, which held that monopoly was a serious flaw in free market economics, since it required the consumer to pay not the optimal price for goods, in which marginal costs were just covered, but whatever price maximized monopoly profits.

In the United States of the 1870s and 1880s the tendency toward corporate control of manufacturing, creating monopolies or trusts that could control an entire industry, led to a public outcry, forcing antitrust legislation. This legislation attempted to make the pursuit of monopoly illegal, using the power of the state to force at least a bare minimum of competition in industry and commerce. The Sherman Antitrust Act of 1890 made illegal trusts and other combinations that aimed to create monopolies and thereby restrict the interstate commerce protected by the U.S.Constitution.

The antitrust laws never succeeded in restoring to industry the kind of competition of many small firms envisaged by Adam Smith. They did, however, counter the worst tendencies toward creating monopolies and restricting trade. Antitrust legislation earned the approval of classical economists and the support of consumers, small businesses, and farmers. In the years following the Sherman Act a number of legal challenges broke up such trusts as Standard Oil.

Observers have noted, however, that the antitrust laws have had little success in combating the concentration of economic activity. About two-thirds of industrial production in the United States today is controlled by large corporations, and the situation is the same in other countries. Today, however, there is significant competition in most industries.

Protectionism and imperialism
Despite such difficulties, capitalism continued to expand and prosper almost without limit throughout the 19th century. It was successful because it demonstrated an enormous ability to create new wealth and to raise the real standard of living for many of those touched by it. As the century closed, capitalism was the dominant economic and social system.

The industrial growth of the 19th century fed into commerce and trade. Overseas trade grew dramatically: world shipping tonnage rose from 4 million to 30 million tons, with European vessels carrying most goods. Increased production stimulated trade in raw materials. The mechanization of European textile production led to a rise in U.S. exports of raw cotton, for example. After 1850 trade in grain, meat, and wool also expanded. Europe became an importer of wheat from North America, Australia, Argentina, and India, paying for imports with industrial exports.

The great surge of European imperialist activity in the second half of the 19th century, especially after 1870, came about largely as a

HIS FAVORITE REMEDY.

result of industrialization. To Europe's empires in Asia were added virtually all the regions of Africa as Britain, France, and Germany emulated earlier colonization by countries such as the Netherlands and Portugal. In Asia Britain absorbed India, completing a process begun by the East India Company in the mercantilist 18th century (*see* page 35). It colonized Sri Lanka (then Ceylon) and Myanmar (Burma), where tea and rubber estates were developed, and took over the Malay Peninsula, which after 1850 saw a rapid expansion of tin mining. France seized Indochina—Vietnam, Cambodia, and Laos; the Netherlands already governed the East Indies; and the United States took the Philippines. In the Pacific Britain colonized Australia and New Zealand, while France claimed Tahiti, and Germany the Marshall, Caroline, and Mariana Islands. Western nations also forced the opening through warfare and aggressive diplomacy of previously closed markets in China and Japan.

The role of colonies
Industrial nations used colonies to supply raw materials and to provide markets reserved for the mother country's products. The colonies

ABOVE: John D. Rockefeller swallows the world with a dose of oil in this cartoon from 1903. Rockefeller's Standard Oil came under harsh criticism for its attempts to achieve a virtual monopoly in the United States.

Henry George and land ownership

In 1897 the American social philosopher and economist Henry George published his book *Progress and Poverty*. In the work George advocated a radical innovation, the single tax. According to George's suggestion, the state would establish all taxes except for a single duty that would take all income that was derived from owning or using bare land; the duty would not affect any income that people derived from improving or working the land.

George's book appeared at the end of a deep depression that had affected the United States from 1873 to 1878. It received a popular reception from an American public profoundly discontented with the apparent realities of an economic life in which the wealth of the few seemed to grow ever higher at the cost of the many. The book sold well and was translated into many languages; George's frequent magazine articles and lecture tours maintained the level of international interest in his plan.

Behind George's proposal lay the remarkable demographic and geographic development of the United States during the 19th century. He pointed out how landowners had grown rich as the frontier of America moved forward, the population increased, and economic development proceeded. He argued, first, that everyone had an equal right to the use of the land. Second, he proposed that the land that had increased in value did so largely as a result of the growth of the community. Its value, therefore, was socially created.

The unearned gain in land values did not derive from the hard work or intelligence of the landowner, but was acquired in an effortless fashion thanks to the general advance of population and industry across the interior of the nation. The fact that landlords received most of the socially created value of land was, in his view, the basic cause of the social unfairness in modern society. George proposed to retain private ownership but believed that society should be the beneficiary of the socially created value of land, leaving landowners to enjoy only the full value of any improvements they might make on the land.

To achieve this end, therefore, George proposed that the socially created value of the land should be taxed away. George's case relied heavily on its humanitarian and religious appeal to a more equable system of landownership. He argued that it made economic sense, too. The government's annual income from the single tax would easily be large enough to pay for the expansion of public works, stimulating employment and relieving poverty.

Although well received, George's work had no significant practical result. Few other economists were prepared to risk their reputations by supporting it. Critics attacked the proposition on the grounds that it appeared to overlook the fact that increasing land values were not the only forms of effortless enrichment: in fact, investors in all kinds of business

enterprises enjoyed similar benefits. Some people questioned why taxation should discriminate against those people who had bought land rather than those who had bought shares in railroads or steel mills, for example.

Indirectly, George's work had considerable influence. It was partly as a result of his legacy that the U.S. government made the lasting commitment to the public ownership of land in the form of America's national parks. George's demand for equal opportunity and his systematic of the economy of rural America also provided the basis for future property regulation.

George's legacy reflected a romantic spirit well suited to this unusual economist: after going to sea as a child, he had been to the gold rush in California, become involved in Democratic politics, and become a newspaper proprietor. On two occasions he ran for mayor of New York City. Although he may have overstated his case, there was some truth in George's assertion that the free, independent spirit, the energy and optimism that marked people in America, are not the causes of geographic expansion, but its results: the American character was shaped by open, unfenced land. Beyond his campaign for land reform George upheld the capitalist system and was an advocate of free trade. His systematic denunciations of social injustices, however, influenced many people who in the early years of the 20th century came to promote socialism.

RIGHT: *Henry George, photographed in the 1880s, once wrote "Political Economy… as currently taught is hopeless and despairing. But this is because she has been degraded… her protest against wrong turned into an endorsement of injustice."*

LEFT: A mechanized reaper on the Great Plains in 1891. Improved agricultural techniques and methods of food preserving improved the diet of most western countries in the late 19th century.

also controlled strategic points, such as the Suez Canal, and provided bases to keep ships and troops supplied all over the globe.

By the end of the 19th century, the primary producing regions were no longer the most important outlets for the products of European and North American industry. Industrial nations became each other's principal customers, and commerce between the Americas and Europe became highly varied. This was largely because industrialized nations had populations that could afford more goods and services. The opposite was true for the primary producing regions of Africa, Asia, and Latin America. There, many nations had become part of European colonial empires, and now nearly all came to depend heavily on a few foreign markets.

Scramble for Africa

Until the 1870s Britain held a clear advantage among industrial nations in international affairs. By 1871, however, Germany and Italy had become unified nations, while France, defeated in the Franco-Prussian War (1870–1871), saw colonial ventures as a way to regain national pride. In 1885 the first chancellor of Germany, Otto von Bismarck (1815–1898), called a conference to discuss how European countries should acquire African colonies. Each country had to give the others "proper notice" of what territory it claimed. Thus began the so-called Scramble for Africa.

The new interest Bismarck sparked in imperialism spread to France. Britain suddenly faced competition, realizing that if it did not seize territories in Africa, the Germans or the French would, depriving it of markets while increasing their own. Britain also believed that it risked losing the colonies it already had to Germany and France.

Depression in Europe in the 1870s and the 1880s led many British observers to believe that markets were scarce because they were

BELOW: Yosemite Valley, in California, originally became a state park in 1864. In 1890 it became the first national park, a development partly reflecting Henry George's philosophy that the land belonged to all Americans.

being taken over by other countries, especially Germany. If the other powers cut Britain off from foreign trade, it would lose its economic position and possibly its empire. In 1883 the British divided the Niger with France; the next year, after Germany claimed Togo and Cameroon as protectorates, the British too began claiming colonies in earnest.

Reaction against classical economics

The industrialization of the 19th century created numerous economic phenomena that appeared to conflict with classical economics. A basic doctrine of classical economists, for example, was Say's law of markets, expounded by French economist Jean-Baptiste Say (1767–1832). Say's law holds that the danger of unemployment or of a glut of goods is negligible in a competitive economy. Supply tends to create matching demand, he argued, up to the limit of human labor and the natural resources available. Each enlargement of output adds to the wages and other incomes needed to purchase added output. Fluctuations apparent in the business activity of industrial nations, however, appeared to conflict with Say's law, reflecting periods of an overall excess of supply, general overproduction, and a clear shortage of demand and purchasing power.

Boom and bust

Capitalist economies, it seemed, were beset by cycles of boom and bust: periods of expansion and prosperity were followed by economic collapse and waves of unemployment. The classical economists who refined the ideas of Adam Smith had no ready explanation for the ups and downs of economic life; they saw such cycles as the inevitable price of the material progress experienced under capitalism. The fluctuations were long seen as temporary aberrations: the basic relationship between employer and worker, between land, capital, and labor, was unchanging. Changes could and did occur in the supply of labor and capital, but they were resolved in the long run in a new, yet similar, equilibrium. The purpose of economic science was to identify the equilibrium, so the classical tradition was a kind of equilibrium economics.

Another problem classical economists had to address was the extreme disparity between the wages and living standards of the workers and those of their employers, the capitalists, and the related unequal distribution of power in the system. The received view, formulated by Ricardo, was that poverty was due to the law of diminishing returns as increasing numbers of workers were added to the productive apparatus, and due also to the high birthrate among workers (*see* page 45). Only toward the end of the century did it become apparent that contrary to the Malthusian theory that

ABOVE: Tourists in Egypt pose at the Suez Canal as a ship passes behind them in the 1890s. The canal, which opened in 1869, linked the Mediterranean and Red Seas, cutting weeks off the sea voyage from Europe to Asia.

influenced Ricardo, as manufacturing wages rose above subsistence levels, there was a decline in the urban birthrate.

Classical economists recognized the huge difference in wealth between employers and workers, but took it for granted. The wealthy, they claimed, were not responsible for the misfortunes of the poor. Following Thomas Malthus (*see* page 45), they held that the low wages of the workers arose from population pressure and were thus their own doing.

Utilitarianism

An earlier defense of the classical system had come from a doctrine called utilitarianism, expressed most notably by British philosopher Jeremy Bentham (1748–1832). Defining utility as the maximization of pleasure or happiness—the greatest happiness of the greatest number—the utilitarians equated such maximization with the production of goods, the undeniable achievement of the new industrialism. Whatever encouraged production, therefore, was beneficial even though it might result in the suffering of the minority. Moreover, the pursuit of happiness was best served when government or social interference was at a minimum.

John Stuart Mill accepted the hardship the utilitarians saw as necessary for progress, but argued that the situation would rectify itself. He believed that an economic equilibrium less hostile to labor would eventually emerge, as in fact happened.

The limitations of liberalism

The early days of the Industrial Revolution were notorious for the appalling conditions suffered by large numbers of workers. Child labor, long working hours, dangerous machinery, and unhealthy workplaces were commonplace. Laborers in all spheres of production became increasingly subject to the demands of larger industrialists or merchants for either credit or work. More often than not, there was no security against unemployment, and social agitation was the only means of protest available.

Liberal opinion makers, such as British free-trade reformer John Bright (1811–1889), argued against any legislation to improve conditions on the grounds that legislation would infringe the subject's liberty, and that society, particularly its economy, would flourish best when it was regulated least. Throughout the 19th century economic liberalism continued to be characterized by a negative attitude toward state authority.

The working classes began to suspect that liberal philosophy protected the interests of powerful economic groups, particularly manufacturers, and that it encouraged a policy of indifference or even brutality toward the laborers. These classes, which had begun to fight for political status and were becoming organized, adopted a political liberalism that was more concerned with their needs.

Emergence of socialism

Anticapitalist movements had a long history. A group calling themselves the Diggers had emerged during the English Commonwealth (1649–1660). The Diggers urged the abolition of private ownership of land and proposed a social system founded on communistic principles. The movement was one of the influences leading to the development of radical thought in the 19th century.

BELOW: The British chief commissioner on Africa's Gold Coast meets a group of Ashanti kings in Accra around 1910. The European scramble to amass African colonies at the end of the 19th century saw virtually the whole continent fall under European political and economic control.

Imperialism and antiimperialism

The late 19th century witnessed a new burst of imperialism as European powers and the United States sought to gain political and economic control over the remaining independent regions of Asia and Africa. The results of the scramble were spectacular. Among other colonial powers, Britain added 4 million square miles and 88 million people to its empire between 1870 and 1898; France nearly the same area and 40 million people; and Germany, itself only unified since 1871, a million miles and 16 million subjects.

The roots of imperialism were varied. Politically, colonies provided a form of national status. Some imperialists argued that it was necessary to take control of strategic states or regions elsewhere in the world to guarantee security; some people argued that the countries of the west had a moral duty to "liberate" other peoples from tyranny and teach them the benefits of western culture and the Christian religion.

One of the most potent arguments in favor of building an empire was economic. To its supporters imperialism was a sensible, possibly even inevitable extension of a mercantile doctrine that emphasized increasing an economy's trade. Colonies, in this argument, provided natural resources to supply the mother country's industries, and the colonies' populations provided a ready-made market for the mother country's manufactured output. Colonial powers passed laws preventing colonies from trading with any other partners and forcing them to use merchant ships from the home nations.

ABOVE: French troops march into Abomey, in modern Benin in 1892. France steadily expanded its possessions in western Africa during the late 19th century.

Some economists, however, argued that although imperialism might seem like common sense, it in fact benefited neither the mother country nor the colony as a whole, but only tiny elites. James Mill, father of economist John Stuart Mill, called the colonies "a vast system of outdoor relief for the upper classes."

At the end of the 19th century another economist warned about the dangers of reckless imperial expansion leading to war. John A. Hobson (1858–1940) was an economic outcast, having previously formulated a theory that attributed the periodic slumps that affected the market to oversaving. Hobson's reasoning that saving left the economy with too little capital to purchase all its output contradicted all economic tradition. Governments still based their policies on accumulating gold and silver; social reformers exhorted workers to thrift, or saving their money.

Eschewed by the economic community, Hobson found himself in South Africa during Britain's imperialist war against the Boer settlers. In *Imperialism* (1902) Hobson brought together his theory of saving with imperialism. He argued that capitalism might one day destroy the world in war through its relentless tendency to expansion and conquest. Hobson argued that a capitalist economy must consume everything it produces, with a buyer for every good. Capitalism distributes money unequally, however. The poor do not have money to buy enough goods, whereas the rich have too much money to buy enough goods. Unable to consume their income, the rich were thus forced to save and, in order to put those savings to use, to invest them. Investment at home, however, would create even more goods that the market could not consume. So they invested it abroad. Imperialism was thus "the endeavor of the great controllers of industry to broaden the channel for the flow of their surplus wealth by seeking foreign markets and foreign investments to take off the goods and capital they cannot use at home."

In Hobson's view this sordid economic competition would, possibly, lead to war between competing nations. Largely ignored by mainstream economists, Hobson's work set the tone for ever more pessimistic views of imperialism. In Marxist theory, for example, imperialism was taken as a sign of the decay of capitalism and the inevitability of world revolution.

Jean Baptiste Say

Jean Baptiste Say (1767–1832) adopted and organized Adam Smith's doctrines in France. One of Say's particular contributions to classical economics was to stress the value of the entrepreneur, who exploits economic opportunity and is the motive force for change and improvement. But Say's most influential contribution was his law of markets. This law proposes that the sum of the values of all commodities produced is always equivalent to the sum of the values of all commodities bought. From the price of every product sold comes a return as wages, interest, profit, or rent sufficient to buy that product. In Say's interpretation of the market, therefore, there can therefore be no underuse of resources: supply creates its own demand.

Classical economic theorists accepted Say's Law despite the evidence of the recurrent crises and depressions that signified its failure. To explain such slumps, they proposed a wavelike business cycle that caused temporary dislocation in the balance of the economy but did not alter its fundamental condition. It was not until the Great Depression of the 1930s that Say's Law was seriously challenged by British economist John Maynard Keynes. Keynes argued persuasively that in direct contradiction to Say's Law, the market could indeed suffer from a shortage of demand. Goods could remain unsold, and their makers unemployed or bankrupt, if consumers had a preference for holding on to money. Corrective action needed to be taken by the government through borrowing and spending to supplement the flow of demand.

Once Say's Law was set aside, it became evident that governments could act directly to implement monetary and or fiscal policies to increase or diminish income and purchasing power. The study of variables such as aggregate demand became known as macroeconomics, which deals with the entire economy; the study of smaller economic units, such as individual consumers or firms, became known as microeconomics.

During the earlier 19th century radical intellectuals in a number of countries objected to capitalism on moral and practical grounds. Among early socialist thinkers were the French aristocrat, Claude de Saint-Simon (1760–1825), and a Welsh mill-owner, Robert Owen (1771–1858) (*see* box, page 69). Other calls for reform came from French philosophers Charles Fourier (1772–1837), a utopian socialist, and Pierre Joseph Proudhon (1758–1823), the father of anarchism.

In the second half of the century socialism emerged as a reaction against the abuses of unrestrained capitalism, such as child labor. Workers began to form labor unions and cooperatives that enabled them to participate in political activities and to protect themselves by political and economic means.

Class differences

Critics of capitalism analyzed the industrial society and proposed social and industrial reforms from both moral and practical standpoints. In moral terms, they claimed, capitalism was unjust: it exploited and degraded workers, and enabled the rich to get richer while the workers faced misery. In practical terms they maintained that the cyclical crises characteristic of capitalism, caused by overproduction or underconsumption, made it an inefficient way of developing society's productive forces. Capitalism did not provide work for all but allowed human resources to be unused or underutilized and produced luxuries instead of necessities. Socialism opposed the liberal emphasis placed on individual achievements and private rights at the expense of collective welfare.

The Swiss economist Jean Charles Sismondi (1773–1842) was probably the first person to draw attention to the fact that society's main classes, the rich and the poor, the capitalists and the workers, had different interests that inevitably put them in conflict with each other. Sismondi argued that the rich were the enemy of the poor and that it was the duty of the state to prevent men being sacrificed to the progress of wealth from which they would derive no profit. Such a view of capitalism reached its peak in the work of the Germans Karl Marx (1818–1883) and Friedrich Engels (1820–1895), the founders of communism (*see* box, page 70). They argued that the workers would eventually rise up and overthrow the capitalists in violent revolution and seize control of the means of production.

ABOVE: A sketch from the mid–19th century shows a group of unemployed men eating in a workhouse. Many workhouses provided only minimal comforts, reflecting a common 19th-century view that laziness made the poor responsible for their own poverty.

LEFT: The consequences of rapid industrialization: a slum in the British coal port of Newcastle-upon-Tyne in 1889. Unsanitary, crowded living conditions were the lot of many of Europe's industrial workers.

Reformism versus revolution

With hindsight, the antagonistic view of class conflict espoused by communism in general and Marxism in particular failed to realize that capitalism itself might seek a compromise with the forces threatening to destroy it. In modern advanced industrial countries, for example, the Marxist revolutionary impulse has been blunted by the provision of reforms and welfare measures. The emergence of government macroeconomic policy in the 20th century and the rise of the corporation, often a multinational, has often left no clear revolutionary target for disaffected workers to attack. In addition, Marx's prediction that the state would "wither away" after being taken over by the proletariat has been thoroughly discredited by the evidence of oppressive bureaucratic power in countries that have experienced the communist experiment in the 20th century.

Reactions to industrialized society

As the 19th century passed, the attention of economic theorists shifted away from cost and supply as the determinants of price and concentrated instead on desire and demand. Adam Smith and the classicists had failed to solve the problem of the difference between value in use—how useful something is—and value in exchange, or how much someone will pay for it. This difference results in the fact that the most precious things, such as water or air, often have a low price. In the 1870s this problem was separately addressed by William Stanley Jevons (1835–1882) in

Social Darwinism

At the heart of much later 19th-century thinking lay an influential doctrine known as social Darwinism. Based on the underlying principles of the theory of evolution articulated by the British naturalist Charles Darwin, social Darwinism explained the development of history, society, economics, and demographics in terms of the survival of the fittest. This famous phrase, which means that the finest specimens of each species are those that will pass on their genes, was first used not by Darwin himself, as many people think, but by the British philosopher Herbert Spencer (1820–1903).

Spencer and his supporters extended Darwin's ideas about biological evolution to human society and even to the rivalry between nations and people. In such a view an economic system like capitalism would comprise some people, the "fittest," who would advance, prosper, and "survive." In contrast, inevitably, the system would also contain victims. Through nobody's fault, but due to a kind of evolutionary inevitability, such people would be the poor and destitute, or the working classes.

Social Darwinism, in other words, presented the inequality and hardship of the capitalist system as an inherent part of its nature. The fortunate and affluent need have no sense of guilt about the inequality of the system because nature had selected them as part of an inevitable process to an improved world. Likewise, there was little point in the better off attempting to alleviate the conditions of the poor or in the poor attempting to better themselves. Superiority and inferiority were innate and unalterable.

Spencer's views had great influence. Applied to countries, for example, social Darwinism justified imperialism as the inevitable weeding out of "lesser" by "superior" peoples. The invidious nature of the doctrine became clear in Germany under the Nazis (1933–1945), when racial "superiority" became the justification for the persecution and extermination of the Jews.

RIGHT: *Charles Darwin is pictured with an ape's body in this 1860 cartoon mocking his theory of evolution.*

England, Karl Menger (1840–1921) in Austria, and Léon Walras (1834–1910) in France. They came up with the theory of marginal utility.

Marginal utility was defined as the extra satisfaction felt by a consumer from a small increment in the consumption of a commodity. It was not the possession of the whole product that conferred value, but the last unit in a series of similar units of a product that the consumer believed was worth acquiring. Marginal analysis was believed essential to rational economic decision-making, whether by individual consumers or producers.

At the heart of the theory of marginal utility was the idea that the value, or utility, of a good or service diminishes with its increasing availability. A hungry person greatly values a slice of bread and is prepared to pay accordingly. He or she probably values a second and a third slice of bread almost as much, but having satiated his or her hunger, will not pay as much for the fourth and fifth slice. A point is finally reached beyond which no further effort at acquisition will be deemed worth making.

Neoclassicism

The consistent application of the idea of marginalism marked a dividing line between the classical theory of Smith and his followers and modern economics. The classical political economists saw the economic problem as that of predicting the effects of changes in the quantity of capital and labor on the growth rate of the national output. The marginal approach of the so-called neoclassical economists, however, focused on the conditions under which these factors tend to be allocated to gain optimal results among their competing uses in the sense of maximizing consumer satisfaction.

The neoclassicists replaced the labor theory of value with a marginal utility theory of

value. According to classical tradition, the cost of production was the sole or principal determinant of goods' market value. Such an approach finally came to be seen as inadequate because it failed to give sufficient weight to difference in value between different kinds of labor and to subjective factors determining individual demands for a commodity.

Economists realized that the demand for particular commodities also affects the value of labor and capital involved in their production. The cost of labor and capital in producing a commodity may temporarily keep the price of the commodity at or above cost. In the long run, however, a persistent lack of demand will force a reduction in labor and capital costs in order to lower the price to the point at which demand will be stimulated.

Alfred Marshall

British economist Alfred Marshall (1842–1924) was a powerful force in the new neoclassical economics. The classical authors, Marshall argued, had concentrated on the supply side of the market, or how items were produced. Marginal utility theory was concerned with the demand side, or what consumers want to buy. Prices are determined by both supply and demand, however. Marshall explained demand using the principle of marginal utility and supply using the rule of marginal produc-

tivity, the productivity of the last unit of a factor of input, such as labor or a new machine, added to the production process.

He explained that in competitive markets, consumer preferences for low prices of goods and seller preferences for high prices were adjusted to some mutually agreeable level. At any actual price, then, buyers were willing to purchase precisely the quantity of goods that sellers were prepared to offer. A market brings together those who are demanding a good or service and those supplying it, with price acting as the pivotal coordinating device. The price at which the amount demanded and the amount supplied are equal, or are in balance, is called the equilibrium price.

How does the market coordinate changes or disturbances in the conditions of demand and supply? Marshall wrote that when demand and supply are in stable equilibrium, if any outside variable should unbalance the equilibrium, forces will come into play that will tend to push it back to a new or the same equilibrium price. If, for example, a war in the Middle East reduces supplies of oil, suppliers will raise their prices because demand exceeds supply. Higher prices will in turn reduce demand, however. Thus the increase in oil prices serves to equalize the market by increasing supply and reducing demand. In the neoclassical model any disturbance to

ABOVE: Londoners gather at a Chartist meeting in 1848. The Chartists, who were influential in the emergence of the labor movement, demanded universal suffrage—the right of all people to vote—and improved working conditions.

Robert Owen

ABOVE: *Children of employees at Owen's factory at New Lanark stage a country dance for visitors. Owen placed great emphasis on education.*

Robert Owen (1771–1858), a Welshman of humble origins, became an important factory-owner in Scotland when he was in his 20s. At his cotton mill at New Lanark Owen's experiments in increasing productivity and profit through improving his workers' environment gained him international fame as a philanthropist who managed to achieve high production while avoiding the worst social abuses of the capitalist system. The improvement of an individual's personal environment, Owen believed, was the key to the advancement of humanity, and at New Lanark he created an environment that reflected this philosophy. Wages were higher and hours shorter than was common; young children were kept out of the workplace and sent to school; and employees lived in better housing than their contemporaries. Yet the mill still operated at a substantial profit.

In this way Owen showed that it was possible to improve factory conditions and make profits at the same time. His campaign for reform of working conditions led to the 1819 act of Parliament forbidding the employment of children under nine.

Modern trade unions were then beginning to develop in Britain, and Owen sought to organize them into a national movement. His aim was to improve working conditions as well as effect basic social and economic reforms. In 1825 he sought to extend his theories concerning human labor as the natural standard of value and purchased land in Illinois and Indiana as a site for a model communal village he called New Harmony. The experiment was a failure, however, and within three years New Harmony had become a shadow of its utopian concept. Owen sold the land at a loss of four–fifths of his total fortune.

In his later years Robert Owen wrote extensively about his theories and took part in numerous socialist congresses. His ideas bore fruit in the international cooperative movement, launched at Rochdale, northern England, in 1844.

markets inevitably gives rise to price changes and hence other responses that serve to bring demand and supply back to equilibrium.

As in markets for consumer goods, reconciliation between supply and demand could occur in markets for money and labor. In money markets the interest rate matched borrowers with lenders. The borrowers expected to use their loans to earn profits larger than the interest they had to pay. Savers, on the other hand, demanded a price for postponing the enjoyment of their own money.

A similar accommodation had to be made in wages paid for labor. In competitive labor markets wages represented at least the value to the employer of the output attributed to hours worked and at least acceptable compensation to the employee for the tedium and fatigue of the work.

Throughout the last three decades of the 19th century the English, Austrian, and French contributors to the marginal revolution largely went their own ways. William Jevons demonstrated the relationship between utility and value in mathematical terms. He argued that one commodity will exchange for another in such a way that the ratio of the prices of the two commodities equals the value of their marginal utilities. Jevons was a founder of econometrics, the use of mathematical methods and models to analyze economic factors.

The Austrian and French schools

The Austrian school of economics under Karl Menger dwelled on the importance of utility, or usefulness, as the determinant of value. Menger argued that exchange takes place because individuals have different subjective

Marxism

Karl Marx developed the idea of class struggle to a point where it posed the most serious challenge to the equilibrium theory of the classical liberal economists. Capitalism, Marx maintained, was the result of a historical process characterized by unceasing conflict between classes. Marx had studied philosophy at the Hegelian Center in Berlin, and it was there that he embraced a dynamic view of history developed from the theories of philosopher Georg Wilhelm Hegel (1770–1831). History, and thus economics, was not a static but a dynamic evolutionary process.

Marx's radical views and writings soon brought him into opposition with the authorities, and in 1843 he was forced to flee Germany for Paris, where he began a close association with the German industrialist Friedrich Engels. In 1849 he settled in London, where he remained until his death in 1883. Marx maintained that capitalism was a stage in an evolutionary process that led from primitive agricultural economy, through feudalism, to a future state that would see the elimination of private property and the class structure. The class structure of a capitalist state reflected the split between those who owned capital and those who did not. By creating a large class of propertyless workers, capitalism was sowing the seeds of its own overthrow by a communist society.

By the end of the 19th century Marxist socialism had become the ideology of many radical political parties in Europe. The transformation of socialism from a doctrine held by a relatively small number of mainly middle-class intellectuals and activists into the ideology of political parties whose membership was largely working-class coincided with the industrialization of Europe and the formation of a large proletariat, a class of workers who survived only by selling their labor.

Marx did not question the productive achievements of the capitalist system. During its rule of scarcely one hundred years, he wrote, it had created more massive and more colossal productive forces than had all the preceding generations together. It was the highly unequal distribution of power and income between workers and capitalists that demanded attention. This inequality was due to the fact that the capitalist took for himself the surplus value accrued by the nonmarginal workers, that is, the workers whose contribution to earnings exceeded the cost of their wages.

Marx shared with classical economists such as Adam Smith and David Ricardo a labor theory of value, which said that the amount of labor used in the manufacture of a product was a key determinant of the product's cost. Marx argued, however, that the capitalist expropriated the surplus value that arose from the difference between what the worker was paid and what he or she contributed to the value of the product. Competition and the desire for wealth would force capitalists to drive wages further down and to invest in labor-saving machinery. Profits would tend to fall at first, until the machinery had paid for itself, and this in turn would lead to an increasing concentration of economic activity in the hands of fewer individuals as they battled to destroy their competitors by outselling them. It would also lead to a growing army of unemployed.

Centralization of the means of production and socialization of labor, Marx wrote, would reach a point where workers became incompatible with capitalism. The result would be the overthrow of the system by a workers' revolution. In Marx's critique the distribution of power was one of the vulnerable points of capitalism. The worker came to the factory with nothing to sell but his or her labor, maintaining the power of the capitalist.

The power of the capitalist had developed from the long association of power with the aristocratic, landowning classes. In accordance with classicism Marx argued that the marginal wage set the wage for all, as dictated by the law of diminishing returns. The value created by those who contributed more worth to a process than they were paid created a surplus value that was rightly theirs but had been stolen by the capitalist.

Marx failed to see that reforms within the capitalist system might avoid the confrontation between capitalist and worker he saw as inevitable, even though he advocated reforms to alleviate the misery of the workers. Many of these reforms have occurred, partly through the operations of welfare capitalism. In addition, Marx failed to realize that the productive power of the capitalist system might contribute toward the benefit of the producing classes, who desired the goods it created.

BELOW: Karl Marx's grave in Highgate Cemetery, London, is still a popular site for his supporters to visit.

ABOVE: Friedrich Engels was a German industrialist whose study of workers' conditions in industrial England convinced him to work with Karl Marx to formulate the basic principles of communism.

valuations of the same commodity. Economists today believe that Menger placed too much stress on consumption demand in the theory of value, just as classical economists had overemphasized production supply.

Menger's work was developed by Friedrich von Wieser (1851–1926), who was his successor as professor of economics at Vienna. Von Wieser also formulated the concept of opportunity costs. Opportunity cost, an essential part of economic decision-making by both consumers and producers, is the value that must be given up to acquire something: for instance, the interest rate that could be earned on a sum of money is given up when that money is instead spent on new plant. When consumers choose commodity A over commodity B, they believe that commodity A will provide greater satisfaction. The sacrifice of commodity B is the opportunity cost.

Walras and equilibrium

French marginalist Léon Walras (1834–1910) described the economic system in general mathematical terms. For each product there is a demand function that expresses the quantities of the product that consumers demand in relation to its price, the prices of other related

goods, the consumers' incomes, and their tastes. For each product there is also a supply function that expresses the quantities producers will supply, this depending on their costs of production, the prices of productive resources (natural resources, capital goods, and labor), and the level of technical knowledge. In the market, for each product there is a point of equilibrium. This idea resembles the equilibrium of forces in classical mechanics: a price exists that will satisfy both consumers and producers.

The point at which equilibrium is possible for a single product can be analyzed. However, equilibrium in one market depends on what happens in other markets, and this is true of every market. There are literally millions of markets in a modern economy, and therefore general equilibrium involves the simultaneous determination of partial equilibria in all markets.

Walras constructed a mathematical model of general equilibrium as a complex system of simultaneous equations. In these equations all prices and quantities are uniquely determined. Walras's economic theory is very abstract, but it offers an analytical framework for incorporating all of the elements of a complete theory of the economic system.

Neoclassicalism today

The neoclassical school continues to dominate economics. Its chief hallmark is a highly systematized, formal, and rigorous method of building models of economic behavior. They are derived from assumptions about the behavior of economic agents—that is, individuals and firms. The tendency of neoclassical economic doctrine has been politically conservative. It advocates competitive markets in preference to government intervention and, at least until the Great Depression of the 1930s (*see* page 93), insisted that the best public policies were those proposed by Adam Smith: low taxes, thrift in public spending, and annually balanced budgets.

Neoclassicists do not inquire into the origins of wealth or describe wealth distribution in moralistic or emotive terms. They explain inequalities in income as well as wealth for the most part in terms of parallel differences among individual human beings in talent, intelligence, energy, and ambition. In other words, men and women succeed or fail because of their individual attributes, not because they are either beneficiaries of special advantage or victims of special handicaps. In capitalist societies neoclassical economics became the generally accepted textbook explanation of price and income determination, although the doctrine was increasingly challenged in the 20th century.

SEE ALSO:

• Volume 5, page 9: Capitalist or free market economies

• Volume 5, page 18: Cooperatives

• Volume 5, page 57: Labor

• Volume 5, page 62: Marginal analysis

• Volume 5, page 100: Socialism

• Volume 5, page 109: Technology

• Volume 5, page 115: Utility

Experiments in planned economics

The 20th century saw the emergence of socialist-inspired economies to challenge the classical tradition of capitalism. The extreme experiments in planned economies failed in various ways, however, sometimes at the cost of great suffering for the people who lived through them.

In a planned economy, unlike a wholly market economy, government intervenes in the production and distribution of a nation's wealth. The 20th century witnessed two major experiments in an extreme form of planned economies, the state-controlled, or "command," economies of the Soviet Union and, later, China. Both achieved varying degrees of success. During the Great Depression of the 1930s, for example, when the capitalist system seemed on the verge of complete failure,

Soviet industrialization seemed to offer a model of a rationally planned economy. The Soviet example was the obvious alternative to the most serious defects of capitalism, such as unemployment, recession, and economic injustice. Command economies brought problems of their own, however, including too much bureaucracy, consumer item shortages, and rationing. By the end of the century all but the most minor communist economies had made concessions to capitalist practices.

ABOVE: Crowds throng a Moscow square to support the revolution of 1917. Lenin's Bolsheviks, although themselves a tiny political party, enjoyed widespread popular support.

LEFT: The Russian revolutionary leader Lenin makes a speech in 1918. An accomplished orator, Lenin was also an influential theorist in the development of Marxist doctrine.

The Russian Revolution

The communist revolution that shook Russia in 1917 initiated an approach to economic planning radically different from the classical economics of the West. Convinced that unfettered capitalism resulted in unfair and inefficient economies, communists believed that government had the responsibility to organize the economy for the good of all its citizens. The economic doctrines of Marx, as interpreted by the Russian revolutionary Lenin, advocated the nationalization of the principal means of production, distribution, and exchange, a centrally directed planned economy, and the collectivization of agriculture.

Karl Marx had predicted that communist revolution would be inspired by industrialization and capitalist exploitation (*see* page 70). In fact, most of the revolutions of the 20th century were sparked by repressive agricultural systems and landlords. The revolution of October 1917 that brought Lenin and the Bolsheviks to power owed much of its success to the dissatisfaction of Russia's huge peasant population. In addition, Russia was disorganized and demoralized by impending defeat in World War I.

After the revolution came civil war, when the communist Red Army fought the counter-revolutionary Whites. Feeding the Red Army and Russia's urban workers presented great problems for Lenin: most of Russia's grain-growing regions were under White control. Lenin sent armed squads into the countryside to seize food from the peasants and independent farmers, called kulaks. Further, Lenin took the whole economy under the central control of the Communist Party. He seized many private factories and directed their production toward the war effort. Railroads, banks, and mines were nationalized, or brought under state ownership. The owners of such businesses received no compensation. Private property, money, belongings: Russians were expected to sacrifice everything for the good of the state.

The results were disastrous. By the end of 1921 production of oil, steel, coal, even shoes, had fallen by over half of its prewar level. Resentful farmers ate their animals and refused to sow new crops, leaving agriculture in chaos. At the end of the civil war in late 1921 peasant uprisings broke out, and factory workers went on strike. An emerging communist leader, Joseph Stalin, put down the uprisings by executing up to two million peasants. Five million more people died from famine.

The New Economic Policy

Lenin introduced a New Economic Policy (NEP) to regain popular support for the revolution. The policy restored some private ownership and allowed peasants to sell what farm produce they had left after they had handed over a certain percentage to the state. Essential industries, such as coal and steel, the transport system, and foreign trade—what Lenin referred to as the "commanding heights of the economy"—remained in state ownership, but many small factories were returned to private ownership to boost industry. By 1928 the measures had restored production

LEFT: *Joseph Stalin, who used cunning and trickery to become the leader of the Communist Party, proved to be one of the greatest tyrants of recent history and was responsible for the murder of millions of Russians.*

levels to those of 1913; in many sectors they were even higher.

After Lenin's death in 1924 Joseph Stalin eventually emerged triumphant in a struggle for the party leadership against Leon Trotsky (*see* box). In 1928, Stalin forced on his country an even more centralized economy, taking in both agriculture and industry. In 1928 he announced a program of forced collectivization that would end private farming by replacing individual farms with state-controlled agricultural villages that would yield cheap crops and a regular source of taxes. Stalin sent troops to force the kulaks into the new villages: many retaliated by burning their crops, causing famine. Between seven and ten million people died as a result of famine or repression; millions were also driven to labor camps in the inhospitable region of Siberia.

The five-year plans

Stalin inaugurated a five-year plan intended to turn the Soviet Union into a world industrial power. Stalin's blueprint for industry gave priority to heavy industries such as steel, coal, and machine manufacture, which formed the basis for other manufacturing. Consumer wants were secondary.

A central agency, Gosplan, set targets for production in every factory and mine. Industrialization found a hero in Alexei Stakhanov. A Ukrainian miner, Stakhanov was required to mine seven tons of anthracite in a shift. In 1935 he and two assistants dug 102 tons in a shift. Stakhanov was publicized as a hero of the revolution. The campaigns to increase output became known as Stakhanovism.

The first five-year plan and the two that followed it—in 1933 and 1938—produced a

BELOW: *A funeral in Russia during the famine of 1921. The famine was almost entirely caused by human action, as farmers and peasants destroyed their crops and animals to protest government attempts to seize them.*

Stalin and Trotsky

Lenin's death in 1924 caused a power struggle at the top of the Communist Party. The adversaries were Joseph Stalin, the Georgian who had risen quickly to become secretary-general of the party, and Leon Trotsky (1879–1940). Trotsky, a Ukrainian Jew, was an intellectual who had led the 1917 revolution with Lenin and organized the Red Army for their outstanding victory in the civil war against the counterrevolutionary Whites. Trotsky was Lenin's own favored successor to the party leadership. On his deathbed Lenin wrote a last testament warning that Stalin should be stripped of his party membership because he was building up a dangerous network of supporters throughout the organization. He saw the Georgian as too rude, incautious, and politically unsophisticated to lead the party. Stalin's supporters suppressed the testament, and Stalin outmaneuvered Trotsky to become leader of the party.

Stalin and Trotsky disagreed fundamentally about the nature of the communist revolution. Trotsky maintained the view, which had been shared by Lenin and the other Bolsheviks, that socialism had to be victorious throughout the world in order to defeat international capitalism. The Soviet Union, Trotsky believed, should take the lead in encouraging revolution in other capitalist countries.

Stalin, on the other hand, supported the principle of what he called "socialism in one country." In other words, the party had to concentrate on making communism a success in the Soviet Union. The rest of the world would then follow the Soviet example. Stalin's view appealed to many ordinary members of the Communist Party, who were eager to set about rebuilding their own country after years of hardship.

Stalin had achieved great popularity among party members, making contacts and carefully recording masses of information about individuals. This tactic earned him the nickname Comrade

ABOVE: *Leon Trotsky at his desk in exile, working on his book called The History of the Russian Revolution.*

Card Index. Stalin's popularity allowed him to set about eliminating all potential rivals.

In 1927 Stalin expelled Trotsky from the party for his opposition to Stalin's plans. Two years later Stalin forced Trotsky into exile. Trotsky traveled to Turkey, France, and Norway before settling in Mexico City. Stalin, meanwhile, organized a series of trials in Moscow accusing Trotsky and others of plotting to overthrow the government of the Soviet Union. In 1940 Trotsky was murdered with an ice pick by an agent believed to have been acting on Stalin's orders.

---

great increase in industrial output. Suppression of the market and centralization of economic decision-making allowed planners to maximize the resources devoted to industrialization. By 1939 the Soviet Union had overtaken Britain as a manufacturing nation, and its industrial capacity lagged behind only those of the United States and Germany. Successful rapid industrialization and the arms industry it supported played a major part in the Soviet Union's ability to defeat the Nazis from 1940 to 1945 in World War II.

By 1950 Soviet output had reached 33 percent of the level of the United States, and by the mid–1970s it was 60 percent. At the end of the 1970s the Soviet economy was 3.5 times larger than Great Britain's. From underdeveloped giant the USSR had become the world's second industrial power.

Industrial progress came at a considerable price for many Russians. Stalin's drive to collectivization and industrialization was accompanied by massive political repression to eliminate all forms of dissent. Millions of

Russians were exiled or murdered. Soviet farming remained much less efficient than agriculture in western Europe or the United States, and shortages were common occurrences. Although centralized economic management of the system encouraged rapid growth, it failed to produce optimal perform-

ABOVE: *Soviet rocket launchers in 1943 . Effective mass production of weapons such as these was a great achievement of the Soviet economy.*

LEFT: A Soviet engineer tests a diesel engine at a factory in Sormov in the 1930s.

ance. The five-year plans tied together a huge part of the economy; the huge interdependence meant that even one subunit could cause overall objectives to be unreachable.

It was also difficult to measure the real effects of the plans. By offering rewards to those who reached, or came close to, their targets, central planners created a temptation to report misleading statistics. Managers often overestimated their requirements of raw material and underestimated their achievable output in order to take more out of the system while putting less in. In their anxiety to meet targets managers responded to the threat of shortages of industrial inputs, including

BELOW: Alexei Stakhanov, the miner who became a hero of Soviet industrial development when he set a record for output, visits Red Square in Moscow in 1947.

skilled labor, by hoarding their resources. Centralization was thus responsible for the development of a sectionalist attitude incompatible with effective planning.

The consequences of state planning

For as long as they enjoyed monopoly status, Soviet producers had little incentive to respond to changes in demand or to improve product quality. This led to overproduction of some goods and shortages of others. Although price controls ensured that there was no inflation, the effect of shortages could be seen in bottlenecks in industrial processes and in empty shelves in stores and shoppers standing in line for provisions. Centralized decision-making, it seemed, had overcome some of the inadequacies of market economies—mass unemployment, severe income inequalities, and dramatic fluctuations in the business cycle—but only by generating a whole new set of problems.

State planning could potentially address the problem of externalities, the side effects of actions involving those not directly a part of the decision-making process, by restricting unsocial activity. In effect, however, the Soviet emphasis on heavy industry led to severe problems with environmental pollution, a negative externality. Factories belched smoke into the air in industrial towns. In the vast regions of Russia the government did little to control such emissions.

State control could also ensure that income was distributed in a form nearer to most people's view of what was just and fair than the market system. However, excessively low prices led to goods being rationed not by

The Chinese Revolution

After the defeat and withdrawal in 1945 of the Japanese military forces that had occupied much of China since 1931, civil war broke out between Chinese Nationalists and Communists, which ended with the proclamation of the People's Republic of China on October 1, 1949. Under its new leader, Mao Zedong, China undertook a large-scale reform of land ownership in a buildup to collectivization, executing many landlords. On other fronts the new Chinese Communist state implemented ambitious health and education programs and forcibly nationalized industry. From then until the death of Mao in 1976 the country went through alternating periods of calm economic development and bouts of radical agitation, such as the Great Leap Forward (1958–1960) and the Cultural Revolution (1966–1969).

their cost but by a lack of supply. Worse, a system in which earnings did not relate to performance and profits did not exist removed motivation from both labor and management.

Finally, the fact that wages and prices differed from free market levels brought not just the industrial process but also the activities of individual citizens under substantial state control. Soviet planners' emphasis on investment in industrial expansion led to the neglect of agriculture, housing, clothing, and other areas of consumer production. The real wages of workers declined and did not regain their 1928 levels until the late 1950s.

Because they could not rely on a rising standard of living as a stimulus to raise levels of labor productivity, economic planners had to try to attain the same ends through persuasion or coercion. The main function of trade unions became to manipulate workers on behalf of the state by raising the level of productivity, improving the quality of production, and reducing production costs. Strikes were forbidden because they were deemed harmful to the interests of the state.

Later, Soviet economic policy-makers began to realize that they had to improve and correct flaws in planning and management if they were to have any chance of maintaining the Soviet Union's high rate of economic growth. A theoretical basis for a more sophisticated approach was provided by mathematicians such as L. V. Kantorovich, who won the Nobel Prize for Economics in 1975. Kantorovich and others suggested ways in which planners could better calculate the allocation

and optimal utilization of natural resources, labor, land, and capital in the production of any given commodity.

China's centralized economy

In 1949 the Communist Party, led by Mao Zedong, seized power in China at the end of a long civil war against the Nationalist Party, or Guomingdang. The communists' first task was to reconstruct a largely rural economy disrupted by decades of domestic warfare. Their basic economic policy consisted of the gradual organization of China's vast number of peasants into agricultural collectives with the intention of promoting efficiency and making savings that would pay for the establishment of heavy industry. The land reform that started in 1950 involved the formation of cooperatives and collective farms.

Private industry was brought under state control meanwhile. In 1953, backed by Soviet aid and technical advice, the Chinese launched their first five-year plan, which allocated resources to heavy industry at the expense of consumer goods. In the urban-industrial sector state ownership of property and commercial enterprises was extended. Industry grew steadily; heavy investment allowed the state-owned sector to achieve complete dominance.

The second five-year plan, which began in 1958, imposed rigid controls on the economy in order to increase agricultural production, restrict consumption, and speed up industrialization. Rural communes—in which land and tools were owned collectively, and farms had

ABOVE: Mao Zedong, leader of China's Communist Party, pictured in a peasant village during the campaign against the Nationalist Party.

LEFT: Chinese students beneath a poster of Chairman Mao read the "Little Red Book," in which Mao outlined his thoughts on communism during the Cultural Revolution of the 1960s.

to meet state planning targets—dominated Chinese farming until the early 1980s. In the industrial sector overinvestment in heavy industry led to serious disruptions in economic management and rational growth.

The five-year plan, which Mao called the "Great Leap Forward," was an economic and social disaster. The Chinese economy became badly disorganized as overinvestment in heavy industry led to upheaval and disruption of rational growth. Between 1959 and 1963 industrial production dropped by as much as 50 percent. Grain output fell by roughly 30 percent between 1958 and 1960. China's death rate doubled, and subsequent estimates have suggested that a largely unnecessary famine killed more than 20 million Chinese in this period.

The Cultural Revolution

In 1966 Mao Zedong launched the "Great Proletarian Cultural Revolution," which was intended to recapture the revolutionary zeal of early Chinese communism. The cultural revolution utterly disrupted Chinese life as Mao's young supporters, the Red Guards, denounced their elders, teachers, and even party leaders for lack of commitment to the revolution. The young set out to end the influence of the belief system that had dominated Chinese government for centuries, Confucianism, which taught respect for tradition and one's elders. City dwellers were subjected to forced relocation to the countryside to provide urban skills in rural areas. The country descended into a state of near anarchy and chaos as the Red Guards became increasingly out of control. Eventually, in 1969 the communist leadership abandoned the policy and set about restoring the economy.

A ten-year plan

After Mao's death in 1976 China's leaders decided to speed up development in all economic sectors to make up for the losses suffered in the preceding ten years. Deng Xiaoping (1904–1999), the dominant figure in Chinese politics in the late 1970s and throughout the 1980s, took a less dogmatic stance on political questions, adopting elements of a market system.

China's reforms restored private peasant agriculture and encouraged private enterprise in an increasingly export-oriented and marketized economy. A ten-year plan for 1976 to 1985 concentrated on improving economic management and giving a larger role to private and collectively owned, as opposed to state-owned, enterprises. Between 1978 and 1984 the share of retail sales controlled by the state sector fell from 90.5 percent to 45.8 percent. A program of incentives devised to increase agricultural production. The agricultural economy was transformed by a system that permitted peasants to sell their surplus at market prices. Since 1978, however, China has been characterized by migration to the thriving cities of peasants from stagnating rural regions of the interior.

In 1979 China relaxed many trade restrictions, enabling increases in foreign investment and trade activity. Special economic zones (SEZs) were established on the southeast coast to encourage rapid business growth by using a system of local tax and incentives to attract Western technology and investment. The first four SEZs, established in 1979, soon became boomtowns; the Chinese government opened 14 more in 1984, followed by another 2 and, in 1992, 23 SEZs in inland China.

Along with increased openness to foreign trade and investment China became part of the international economy, joining the World Bank and the International Monetary Fund in 1980. The result was annual economic growth averaging 10 percent throughout the 1980s.

Economic expansion

The further decentralization of economic planning during the 1980s, foreign investment, and an increased reliance on market forces to determine the prices of consumer goods led to an annual growth rate in the early 1990s of well over 10 percent, the fastest in Asia. This rapid expansion caused some problems, such as high inflation rates in urban areas and increasing economic inequalities between regions and social groups.

Deng Xiaoping resigned in 1990 but retained effective power, touring the special economic zones of southeast China and advocating "capitalist methods" to promote growth. Doctrinaire opponents of economic reform in official posts were replaced, and economic growth continued unchecked. By the mid-1990s more than $90 billion in foreign investment had entered China, and foreign-funded firms were responsible for over 27 percent of China's exports.

A major boost to China's economy came with the return by Britain of Hong Kong in

LEFT: *U.S. president Richard Nixon attends a state banquet in China in February 1972. Nixon's trip was the first sign of closer relations between China and the capitalist world.*

79

LEFT: *An East German worker helps build the Berlin Wall in 1961. The wall was built by the communists to prevent East German workers fleeing to find better conditions in the West.*

1997. The colony, leased by Britain from China in the 19th century, had become renowned for entrepreneurship and mass production of consumer goods. The new Chinese governors encouraged continued business activity, but many citizens of Hong Kong protested against the communists' refusal to allow them any meaningful form of democratic representation.

The Cold War: communism vs. capitalism

After the defeat of Nazi Germany in World War II in 1945 mutual suspicion alienated the Soviet Union—whose troops occupied most of Eastern Europe—from its erstwhile allies in the West. In 1948, for example, the United States excluded the Soviet Union from the $13 billion European Recovery Program, the so-called Marshall Plan, that provided aid to Western European states. The Soviet Union itself sought to install communist-dominated governments in Eastern Europe. The tense standoff between the United States and the Western democracies on the one hand and the Soviet Union and its communist allies on the other was dubbed the Cold War. It dominated global politics for the next four decades.

In Eastern Europe the Russians set about reproducing in each state Soviet-style centralized economic mechanisms and developing bilateral trade relations with, and ultimately economic dependence on, the Soviet Union itself. Moscow's interest was as much strategic as economic: the countries of the so-

called Eastern bloc formed a protective buffer zone against possible Western attack. To sustain these satellites was expensive, however: the Soviet Union had to subsidize energy exports to the communist nations at below world market prices in return for overpriced industrial goods.

COMECON and the Eastern bloc

The formation of the Council for Mutual Economic Assistance (COMECON) in 1949 brought together East Germany, Czechoslovakia, Poland, Romania, Bulgaria, Hungary, and the USSR in a trading bloc that later also included the communist states of Cuba and North Vietnam. With different economic structures, levels of development, technologies, and systems of private ownership, these economies in theory had many opportunities for mutually beneficial multilateral trade. In practice, however, the strategic interests of the USSR dominated COMECON and prevented

such economic interchange. The absence of a properly convertible currency between the economies also seriously hindered satisfactory trade settlements.

In 1956 Hungarians revolted against the ruling communist regime. Soviet troops brutally suppressed the uprising, but the Hungarian government began a process of gradual economic reform, adopting a certain amount of capitalist features to encourage service industries and the production of consumer

ABOVE: Soviet tanks line a street in Prague, Czechoslovakia, during the suppression of the Prague Spring.

The Prague Spring

ABOVE: Angry Czechoslovakians shout their defiance at Soviet troops during the invasion that suppressed the Prague Spring. To gain some credibility for their actions, the Soviets also used forces from other Eastern bloc countries in the invasion.

In 1968 Czech communist leader Alexander Dubček began a series of reforms intended to create "socialism with a human face." Rather than the Soviet style communism imposed by the Russians, he wanted to evolve a form of government with the consent of the people, granting increased freedom to the media and promising economic reform. The reforms were highly popular with ordinary Czechs.

To the Soviet leadership, however, the Czech reforms were a cause of great suspicion. They were anxious that economic reforms might herald a decline in the power of the Communist Party and, eventually, Czechoslovakia's abandonment of the Soviet alliance to join the West. Although the Czech leadership had no such intentions, the Russians decided to intervene. Tanks and troops crushed the Prague Spring on August 20, 1968.

goods. By the time communism collapsed in eastern Europe in 1989 the Hungarian economy had become the most market-oriented in the Soviet bloc.

During the 1960s Soviet economists such as Yevsey Liberman also began to urge the introduction of some features of capitalism into the Marxist economic framework. Using the profit motive, they argued, was the best way to stimulate efficiency and increase industrial production. Senior officials agreed, admitting that current management methods were failing to maximize production capacity. They argued that centralized general direction should employ such measures as cost accounting, production based on demand, and wage incentives.

ABOVE: U.S. president Ronald Reagan and Soviet premier Mikhail Gorbachev at a summit meeting in Geneva in 1985. Gorbachev's policy of reforms and increased openness made him highly popular with Western leaders.

Planned economies in the developing world

Beyond the Eastern bloc the Soviet and Chinese examples inspired other attempts at planned economics in the second half of the 20th century. In 1955, for example, the nationalist president of Egypt, Gamal Abdel Nasser, made an arms pact with the Soviet Union via Czechoslovakia. When the British and United States responded by withholding money to build the Aswan Dam project, Nasser nationalized the Suez Canal in order to raise the money bringing it under state control and angering the British, French, and Israelis, who launched a shortlived invasion. Nasser, though himself politically moderate, launched a policy of "scientific socialism" aimed at state encouragement of industry. Industrial output rose from 10 percent of the GDP in 1950 to 21 percent in 1970. Egypt's agriculture did not keep pace, however, and a period of rapid population growth undermined much of the economic progress.

Nasser's ties with the Soviet Union were impelled by the military danger from Israel. Ironically, Israel itself, created in 1948, also incorporated a high degree of central economic planning. Funded by the United States and other allies, Israel also benefited from a highly motivated population enthusiastic to support a high level of government interference in the economy.

Numerous African countries also experimented with central economic planning, though they were often more directly sympathetic with Soviet ideology than either Egypt or Israel. In Tanzania, for example, Julius Nyerere launched a program of socialist economic development in 1967 called *ujaama*, or familyhood, based on ideas of voluntary cooperation. In Ethiopia, meanwhile, the Marxist-Leninist military government that took power in 1974 used Soviet economic support to establish a program of nationalization of industry and commerce.

Both plans failed. Nyerere's idealism met resistance from peasants and sank under inefficiency and corruption. Huge rises in petroleum costs further ruined the economy. The Ethiopian economy foundered under the cost of fighting rebels in the province of Eritrea and the devastating impact of drought and famine in the 1980s.

In Southeast Asia the Vietnam War ended in victory for the communist North and reunification of the country. In 1976 a plan for recovery called for industrialization in the north and agricultural expansion in the south. Many people, particularly ethnic Chinese from the southern city of Saigon, resisted being relocated to the government's "new economic zones" in rural areas. In 1978 the announcement of a program for the increased socialization of industry and agriculture in the south led to hundreds of thousands of people— mainly ethnic Chinese—fleeing the country. Many became "boat people," putting to sea on tiny, overcrowded craft; many died from drowning or from attack by pirates.

Neighboring Laos followed the Vietnamese model, setting up agricultural collectives and nationalized industry and commerce. In Cambodia the Khmer Rouge government of Pol Pot, which took power in 1975, drove city dwellers out to labor in the countryside and executed millions of Cambodians it considered "intellectuals." The country's economy collapsed entirely before the neighboring Vietnamese invaded to restore order in 1979.

Throughout the economies of Southeast Asia, as with other experiments in economic planning, the 1980s brought concessions to capitalism. Poor economic performance forced governments to adopt market incentives, privatization, and decentralized economic planning to a greater or lesser degree.

LEFT: *The hero of the 1959 Cuban revolution. Fidel Castro led the revolution and became Cuba's leader for the rest of the century.*

The Liberman approach

In October 1965 the Soviet government introduced legislation to implement demand-based production for industry, farms, transport, construction, and communications. Working capital would be assigned to each enterprise, and local management would determine its use. A total payroll was also to be assigned to each enterprise, allowing local management to choose whether to pay workers by time or piecework, and to award pay bonuses based on profits. By mid–1969 enterprises operating under the new system were producing one–third of the total industrial output.

The so-called Liberman approach declined in the early 1970s during a period of political retrenchment in the Soviet Union. In 1968 a new reformist leadership under Alexander Dubček had inaugurated a brief period of liberalization in Czechoslovakia, the so-called Prague Spring (*see* box, page 81). Dubček's reforms were crushed by Russian military intervention due to fears that it would lead to a return to capitalism throughout the entire Soviet Bloc. As a result, the Soviet leader, Leonid Brezhnev, effectively prevented further reform of communism for the following 20 years, the so-called "years of stagnation."

Planned economies in Soviet satellites

Within the Soviet system the Hungarian example was just one variation on the Soviet theme. Yugoslavia, for example, developed its own model of partial market socialism based on workers' self-management in competing enterprises (*see* box, page 85). In 1949, differences between the USSR and Yugoslavia led to the latter's expulsion from COMECON. Yugoslavia turned for financial aid to the West

in the shape of the U.S. Export-Import Bank and the International Bank for Reconstruction and Development. In 1956, however, Soviet premier Nikita Khrushchev made available a Soviet loan of $84 million to Yugoslavia and canceled its outstanding debt of $90 million. By 1963 Yugoslav trade with the USSR and the other communist states was increasing, but 70 percent of the country's trade was still with the West and neutral countries.

Castro and Cuba

In Cuba Fidel Castro assumed power in 1959 and, after failing to establish diplomatic or trade relations with the United States, negotiated arms and credit agreements with the USSR. Castro nationalized resources and collectivized agriculture, angering the United States by seizing U.S.-owned companies. In 1961, after an unsuccessful attempt to overthrow him in the Bay of Pigs Invasion, Castro became openly aligned with the USSR, relying increasingly on Soviet economic and military aid. This led in 1962 to the confrontation between the United States and the USSR known as the Cuban missile crisis. Following the resolution of the crisis, Castro achieved considerable status in the developing world through his leadership of the Nonaligned Movement (*see* page 101).

In the 1970s Castro implemented market reforms based on the model proposed by Liberman, particularly pursuing the self-financing of state enterprises. In 1979 the government set up "resource fairs" where enterprises could buy and sell surplus resources free from government regulation. As the state sector adopted more market principles in the 1970s and 1980s, private entrepreneurs were given freer reign, notably through the establishment of "free peasant markets" in the cities.

When the Cuban rulers grew disenchanted with the free peasant markets in the early 1980s, the "parallel market" was extended to fill the void. The government increased the prices it paid to private commercial farmers in return for extra production for these markets. In the late 1980s, when the USSR began to introduce economic restructuring, Castro retained a hardline Marxist stance. However, with the collapse of the USSR and COMECON in 1990 Cuba's economic problems threatened to become overwhelming.

Crisis and collapse

The "years of stagnation" in the Soviet bloc under Leonid Brezhnev lasted through the 1970s and early 1980s. A slowdown in the USSR's growth reflected not only a lack of dynamism in the economy but also a failure to make the necessary transition from extensive growth, based on mobilizing new resources, to intensive growth, based on increased productivity. With restricted access to Western technology the USSR was poorly equipped to make this change.

The United States and the USSR had maintained massively expensive defense programs through the Cold War period, culminating in a huge arms buildup by U.S. President Ronald Reagan in 1981. It became clear that the Soviet Union, already involved in a costly war in Afghanistan (1980–1989), could not afford the enormous added expense of the new arms race. The Soviet economy was swamped by the burden of defense expenditure. Whereas the United States devoted only 5 or 6 percent of gross domestic product (GDP) to military procurement' the commitment from the USSR's smaller economy was 12 to 15 percent.

Gorbachev's reforms

In 1985 Mikhail Gorbachev became premier of the Soviet Union and launched economic and political reforms to bolster the economy. These reforms, called perestroika, or restructuring, attempted to develop more of a consumer society. Perestroika was overtaken by events, however. The Soviet bloc was unraveling. The opening of the Berlin Wall in November 1989 marked the approaching end of the Cold War and the end of Soviet-style economic activity.

The country began to fall apart with the rise of separatist tendencies, particularly in the Baltic republics of Estonia, Latvia, and Lithuania. Between 1989 and 1991 communist governments lost power in Poland, Hungary, Czechoslovakia, and East Germany. COMECON was disbanded, and in February 1990, with the Soviet economy rapidly deteriorating, the communist party of the Soviet Union gave up its monopoly on power. The crisis of command economies appeared to many observers as further evidence that the decisions of millions of individual consumers through the

market mechanism were better at allocating resources than any form of state interference.

Gorbachev sought to implement further political and economic reforms, but in August 1991 communist hardliners attempted a coup. Although the coup failed, the USSR came to the point of collapse. The influence of Russian Federation President Boris Yeltsin eclipsed that of Gorbachev, and the Russian government assumed the powers previously exercised by the Soviet government. Gorbachev resigned on December 25, and the Soviet parliament acknowledged the dissolution of the USSR on December 26, 1991.

The collapse of communism

Today, the growth of private interests under state-capitalism has prepared the way for private capitalism in the former Soviet Union. Communist Party bureaucrats and enterprise managers have reinvented themselves as entrepreneurs or facilitators in a privatized

Marshall Tito and Yugoslavia

Born near Zagreb, Croatia, on May 7, 1892, Josip Broz Tito was was the effective leader of Yugoslavia from 1943 and its official head of state from 1953 until his death on May 4, 1980. The leader of the communist partisans who helped liberate the country from German occupation at the end of World War II, Tito used his personal authority and popularity to unite the disparate peoples of the Yugoslav federation—Bosnians, Croats, Macedonians, Slovenes, Serbs, and others. The collapse of the region into ethnic hatred and conflict in the decades since Tito's death is testimony to the strength of the authority he exerted to keep the country together.

In economic terms Tito carefully steered Yugoslavia along a middle path between the threats of the Soviet Union on the one side and the blandishments of the West on the other. While U.S. and other Western leaders mistrusted Tito because he was a communist, the Soviet Union feared his independent streak and his country's desire for self-determination.

The crisis came in 1948. Tito's relations with the West had reached their lowest ebb after Yugoslavia had backed the communist side in the Greek civil war. Stalin, meanwhile, expelled Yugoslavia from COMECON, the economic organization of the Eastern bloc. The expulsion was the start of a vigorous Soviet campaign to bring down Tito through a combination of economic blockades, border incidents, and threats of invasion. The effect of Stalin's action was to unite the Yugoslav people even more strongly behind their leader, while Tito encouraged an economic system based on workers' self-management. Elected workers' councils were given authority to run local enterprises.

After the death of Stalin in 1953 his successor, Nikita Khrushchev, built a new relationship with Tito and visited Belgrade in 1955. The Soviet Union formally rejected Stalin's policy of attacking Yugoslavia and acknowledged its right to

ABOVE: Marshall Tito at a rally in Yugoslavia in 1954. Tito's maneuvering kept Yugoslavia independent of either the Soviet or Western blocs.

choose its own road to socialism. Tito's economic reforms barely outlasted him, however. The warfare that struck Yugoslavia after his death effectively stalled economic development.

economy. Stalinism as an ideology of forced industrialization was at an end in Europe. By the end of the 20th century socialism—as represented by the socialist parties—had not only lost its original anticapitalist outlook but was also coming to terms with the fact that capitalism could not be controlled or abolished in individual countries.

Planned economies in the West

The inadequacies of planned economies became increasingly apparent in the last ten years of the 20th century after the collapse of communism. Most economists now generally believe that constrictive planning inhibits productivity and economic development.

A limited element of planning, however, has become common in many of the industrial economies of the West. Such economies combine private ownership of property and business with elements of control—nationalization, subsidies, taxes, and prices and

incomes policies—designed to prevent unfettered competition.

Even in countries like the United States, where outright government ownership is exceptional, government still exerts great influence over economic activity. It uses monetary and fiscal policies to promote growth and stability, is both a producer and a consumer, and imposes regulations that improve the economy. Most economists now accept the concept of a "mixed economy," which combines private initiative with some government control.

In the developed world there is strong opposition to controls and national planning. Nevertheless, in times of emergency, such as during World War II, democratic governments have applied central planning measures without serious opposition. In general, though, free-enterprise economies see state ownership and government interference as undesirable exceptions to private ownership and the determination of price by competitive markets.

SEE ALSO:

• Volume 4, page 63: The world economy

• Volume 5, page 36: Externalities, environmental

• Volume 5, page 100: Socialism

• Volume 5, page 68: Mixed economies

The West in the 20th century

Two world wars, political totalitarianism, and the most traumatic depression the world has known challenged 20th-century economists into reassessing classical and neoclassical theory and, in Keynesianism and monetarism, produced the dominant economic theories of the century.

ABOVE: *Workers on the early production line making the Model T Ford, the first mass-produced automobile. The increase in output achieved by the assembly line allowed Ford to corner half the U.S. automobile market by 1915.*

From the publication of Alfred Marshall's *Principles of Economics* in 1890 until the Wall Street Crash of 1929 economic theory remained relatively stable in capitalist societies. In the Soviet Union after 1917 Lenin reinterpreted Marxist theory to formulate a communist economic doctrine that paralleled and, in the eyes of some people, rivaled capitalism (*see* page 72). In the West, meanwhile, Marshall's neoclassical followers developed, consolidated, and refined the concept of marginal utility, or the satisfaction felt by a consumer from the consumption of an added unit of a commodity.

The theory of utility became applied to the analysis of consumer behavior under many circumstances, such as changes in income or price. The theory led to the interpretation of production in terms of marginal productivity, the cost of producing the last item of a given commodity. With it came a new theory of distribution: wages, profits, interest, and rent were all shown to depend on "marginal value product," the market value of the output generated by one additional unit of a factor of production, such as labor or plant.

Until the worldwide Great Depression of the early 1930s the neoclassical position seemed unassailable to non-Marxist economists in the West. Neoclassicists argued that economic agents, whether individuals or firms, based decisions not on absolutes but on marginal changes. Economic agents sought certain objectives and, to attain them, arranged the best means of doing so. Prices adjusted to marginal costs; costs, including that of labor, adjusted downward as necessary to ensure the employment of all available plant, materials, and above all, workers. Say's Law ruled (*see* page 65): demand was adequately sustained by what was paid out in wages, interest, and profits; prices moved to accommodate any interruption in the return flow of purchasing power.

Neoclassical models of economic behavior assumed that individuals chose goods so as to maximize satisfaction, or utility, while firms were motivated by profit maximization. Price played a key part in coordinating the actions of consumers and producers. The price at which the amount demanded and the amount supplied were equal was called the equilibrium price. Price thus performed the crucial coordinating function in the neoclassical market model.

Neoclassicism and competition

The power of the market to balance the price of a commodity against its marginal cost remained largely theoretical. Neoclassical economists such as Marshall concentrated on two extreme types of market structure: pure monopoly, in which one seller controlled the entire market for one product (*see* box, page 88), and pure competition, characterized by many sellers, many highly informed buyers, and a single standard product. Where there was imperfect competition, however, with either buyers or sellers enjoying an advantage, competition would not drive prices into equality with marginal costs.

An influential contribution to neoclassical theory came in 1911 with the publication of *The Theory of Economic Development* by the Austrian economist Joseph A. Schumpeter (1883–1950). Schumpeter developed a theory of economic growth and fluctuation that took into account the contribution of technical innovation. The central figure in Schumpeter's system, the entrepreneur, challenged the established equilibrium with a new product, process, or type of productive organization. The tendency then was toward a new equilibrium, a new stability in what Schumpeter saw as a circular flow in which production moved in one direction, money in the other. This new equilibrium would inevitably be disturbed by the next innovator and the next change in the productive process. Economic life would continue and enlarge; that was the nature of economic development.

Concentrating on the evolutionary nature of economics, Schumpeter also believed that monopoly, seen as an aberration by classical economists who promoted competition, had a positive role to play in economic life. Classical economists pointed out that monopoly kept prices higher than marginal cost because price pressure from competitors had been removed. Schumpeter argued that innovation was best financed and rewarded when an innovator was freed by monopoly from the threat of imitation or competition. Consumers might therefore benefit from monopoly if the dominating company used its profits as a spur to innovation. Under monopoly capitalism firms would concentrate less on price competition than on technical and organizational innovation, thus sending "gales of creative destruction" through the economic system.

Thorstein Veblen and U.S. economics

A challenge to the neoclassical system of economics came from U.S. economist and social scientist Thorstein Veblen (1857–1929), who at the turn of the century published a series of

87

Revising neoclassicism

Neoclassical theory proposed a marketplace of perfect competition that would be undermined by monopolies or oligopoly interests. Two economists, Edward H. Chamberlin (1899–1967) in the United States and Joan Robinson (1903–1983) in Britain, introduced in the mid–20th century a new idea of monopoly that made it potentially a much larger part of the classical system. They argued that between the classical case of competition, where no single producer controlled price, and the supposedly exceptional case of monopoly, where a single producer could control price so as to maximize return, there actually lay a range of intermediate cases. In some cases this may be more or less complete monopoly, where only one producer supplies the whole market.

In others the market may be an oligopoly, meaning that it is dominated by a handful of major suppliers. Oligopolies then apparent in the market included, for example, the American automobile industry, which had only three major performers, and the petroleum, steel, chemical, rubber tire, machine-tool, and farm-equipment industries.

In contrast with oligopolistic competition, in which there are only a few firms producing a product that is undifferentiated or standard, monopolistic competition is characterized by several firms producing a similar but differentiated product. Chamberlin and Robinson argued that in monopolistic competition a number of firms might all charge a higher price than they would if the industry were perfectly competitive.

In monopolistic competition, therefore, firms compete not just on price but in terms of product differentiation. Producers use branding and packaging, often with the associated techniques of advertising, to distinguish their product in consumers' minds from similar products. A box of detergent, for example, might be more eye-catching than others. Branding and advertising give each producer a partial monopoly, creating enough brand loyalty to ensure that a consumer might continue to buy a particular product even if a producer raises its price above the market level.

Chamberlin and Robinson failed to provide a satisfactory theory of price determination under monopolistic competition. The members of an oligopoly could theoretically achieve a price and profit not significantly different from those of a monopoly. No longer could the socially optimal price and output of the competitive market be assumed. In reality, however, oligopoly aroused little consumer resentment: in most advanced economies monopolistic competition is characteristic of manufacturing industries.

ABOVE: The first Model T Ford, made in 1908. Before the model was discontinued in 1927, more than 15 million had been produced.

influential papers. Veblen considered that the central ideas of neoclassicism were not founded on truth but only approved belief. The carefully calculating, pleasure-maximizing individual proposed by neoclassical economists was an artificial construct; human motivation was far more diverse. Economic life was evolutionary, and so economic theory was wrong to propose static and continuously valid conditions. Just as economic institutions changed, so should economic subject-matter. The unqualified commitment to neoclassical ideas overlooked this fact

In *The Theory of the Leisure Class* (1899) Veblen examined the manners and motives of the rich who dominated U.S. society. He divided society into a "predator," or "leisure," class, which owns business enterprises, and an "industrious" class, which produces goods. Veblen criticized business owners for what he considered their emphasis on gain and characterized the leisure class as a parasitic and harmful influence on the economy.

The Gilded Age

The target of Veblen's criticism, the very wealthy of the so-called Gilded Age of the end of the 19th century, attracted attention and even admiration through their ostentatious expenditure. Families such as the Vanderbilts fascinated many Americans with their reckless spending. Such behavior had received an apparent endorsement from social Darwinism, which equated social status with an innate superiority (*see* box, page 67).

Veblen argued, however, that what he dubbed the "conspicuous consumption" of the rich was useless and potentially harmful. He examined the rich as an anthropological

phenomenon: "The institution of a leisure class," he wrote, "is found in its best development in the higher stages of barbarian culture. The flaunted wealth of the massively rich in modern society mirrors the displays of tribal leaders in primitive societies. Just as tribal leaders set great store by the adornment of their women, so 'the wife' has become the ceremonial consumer of goods which he produces." The attack on the idle rich struck a chord with many Americans, brought up to believe in the virtues of self-sufficiency and hard work.

Veblen's influence

Earlier economists had made consumption the highest purpose of classical economics. Consumption and acquisition provided the supreme source of the "happiness" described by Jeremy Bentham in the 18th century as the goal of all people in an economy. The ability to consume more was the ultimate justification of all effort and toil.

Veblen's contribution categorized consumption in its fullest development as the vacuous gratification of childish personal aggrandizement. Veblen maintained in other writings that the economic system of his day was based on price fluctuations and suggested that the inefficiency of the system could be corrected by placing experts in charge of production and distribution. He saw a conflict between engineers and scientists—skilled and potentially productive—and profit-oriented business people, who suppress the tendencies of such professionals in the interests of maintaining prices and maximizing profits. Veblen also emphasized the ordinary worker's pride in his or her work and scorned the sub-

servience of academics to the business interests that controlled U.S. universities.

Veblen was a strong influence in the school of economic thought known as institutional economics, which flourished in the United States in the 1920s. It included such names as Wesley Clair Mitchell (1874–1948) and John R. Commons (1862–1945) but did not develop a coherent theoretical scheme to replace or supplement orthodox neoclassical theory. Institutional economists were united, however, in their dissatisfaction with the abstract theorizing of orthodox economics, its tendency to cut itself off from the other social sciences, and its preoccupation with the automatic market mechanism.

Ford and the assembly line

The U.S. economy itself changed in the early decades of the 20th century. Large-scale mass production, an increased division of labor, and the growth of credit to facilitate mass consumption characterize a type of capitalism known as Fordism. In 1913 U.S. industrialist Henry Ford (1863–1947) began using standardized interchangeable parts and assembly-line techniques in his motor vehicle plant. Although Ford was not the first person to use such practices, he was chiefly responsible for their general adoption and for the consequent great expansion of American industry.

In Ford's system the mental and manual aspects of work became completely separate. As vehicles passed along a mechanized assembly line, each worker performed one or a small number of repetitive tasks on each vehicle. This represented a considerable break from the past, when production had been organized along the traditional lines of crafts,

Scapegoats

In the decade after World War I the citizens of both victorious and vanquished countries sought scapegoats to explain the economic depression and social hardship they faced. The targets they chose for their resentment varied widely but usually had little basis in reality. In the United States, for example, Attorney-General Mitchell Palmer instituted a "red scare" and expelled many people from the country for their supposed sympathies with communist and socialist theories. The Industrial Workers of the World, called the Wobblies, an international labor organization set up in 1914, was another target of official hostility. U.S. fear of internal threats peaked in 1927 with the execution of the Italian-born anarchists Nicola Sacco and Bartolomeo Vanzetti. Worldwide protests against the execution focused on doubts about the pair's guilt in the murder for which they were convicted and on suspicion that they were being scapegoated for being foreign and holding "un-American" political beliefs.

Socialists and communists were among the most common scapegoats targeted, with or without the tacit support of governments that did not themselves wish to take the blame for economic hardship. Another common scapegoat echoed attitudes from the Middle Ages, when Europe's Jews were singled out as greedy profiteers. In Germany Adolf Hitler's Nazi party encouraged people's resentment with propaganda that, without any objective evidence, depicted Germany's Jews as an enemy within the state. Such attitudes paved the way for the Nazis' later classification of the Jews as "inferior" people and the extermination program that followed.

ABOVE: A French cartoon from World War I shows Jewish businessmen as profiteers, a theme repeated many times after the conflict's end.

with workers possessing skills of organization and operation.

By early 1914 Ford's innovations, although greatly increasing productivity, had resulted in a monthly turnover of labor in his factory of 40 to 60 percent, as workers escaped the monotony of assembly-line work and the increasing demands of their production quotas. Ford doubled the daily wage then standard in the industry from about $2.50 to $5, bringing increased labor-force stability and a substantial reduction in operating costs. Together with the enormous increase in output made possible by new technological methods, these factors led to a doubling of company profits from $30 million in 1914 to $60 million in 1916.

Scientific management

The new mode of production involved the application of increasing mechanization in large, multidepartment firms, moving assembly lines, and standardization of components and finished products. Taylorism, based on principles of "scientific management" developed by U.S. engineer Frederick Winslow Taylor (1856–1915), separated the organizers of production, such as engineers, from the semiskilled operatives who carried out the

production, bringing increased managerial control into the process. There was considerable resistance to such changes, but labor unions eventually accepted them.

Such was the efficiency of production at Ford's plant that cars were made at ever decreasing prices, reaching a minimum of $50. One car left the line every 10 seconds, an annual rate of 2 million. As a result the 1920s brought mass motoring to the United States, with more than 90 percent of world vehicle production. The low price enabled employees to be consumers of their own products, sharing in the gains in productivity and the associated value added through increases in their real wage. In this way Ford matched mass production and technical progress with higher mass consumption.

World war and its aftermath

While American industrialization forged ahead, many other states were suffering the economic consequences of the greatest conflict the world had then seen. World War I (1914–1918) ended in the defeat of Germany and its allies by the United States, Britain, France, and their allies. In Russia the hardship created by the war led in part to revolution in

1917. Led by Marxist communists, the workers toppled imperial rule and took control of the Russian state. Under Lenin (1870–1924) and, from 1924, Joseph Stalin (1879–1953) Russia and later the Soviet Union turned its back on capitalist economics.

The Russian Revolution established Marxist-based communism as a vigorous and hostile competitor to the capitalist system. From 1917 until the Great Depression of 13 years later people in many countries saw the new Soviet economic system as a plausible alternative to the harsh, even inhuman realities of the current economic system. The very occurrence of the revolution, in apparent fulfillment of Marx's predictions, had contradictory effects on economic thinking. The threat of revolution persuaded some economists to urge reform: the introduction of old-age pensions, unemployment compensation, trade union support, and a minimum wage would alleviate the anger of the masses. Other economists judged all such suggested change to be capitulations to the Soviet model and urged instead a yet more rigorous application of free market methods.

Postwar Europe

Among the reasons Russian communism attracted considerable popular support in the United States and other industrialized countries was the threat of the collapse of the capitalist system after the end of the war.

Europe and its economy lay in ruins. The situation was most grave in Germany. The 1919 Treaty of Versailles imposed harsh terms on Germany for its role in the war. Germany lost domestic territory and its colonies; it was made to surrender most of its coal, trains, and merchant ships. Worst of all in the eyes of most Germans, Germany was forced to accept full responsibility for the war and pay reparations, or a fine, for its cost.

The devastated German economy could not meet its reparations requirements. French troops moved into the Ruhr region of Germany in 1923 to take over coalmines and extract the reparations. The German government encouraged the workers to passive resistance, printing vast amounts of money to pay them. This was among the causes of the hyperinflation that saw prices jump 10-billion-fold in a 16-month period. Savings, pensions, insurance, and other forms of fixed income were wiped out, creating a social revolution that destroyed the most stable elements in German society.

The cost of victory

The situation was almost as bad for the war's victors. In France the most pressing domestic problem at the end of the war was the stabi-

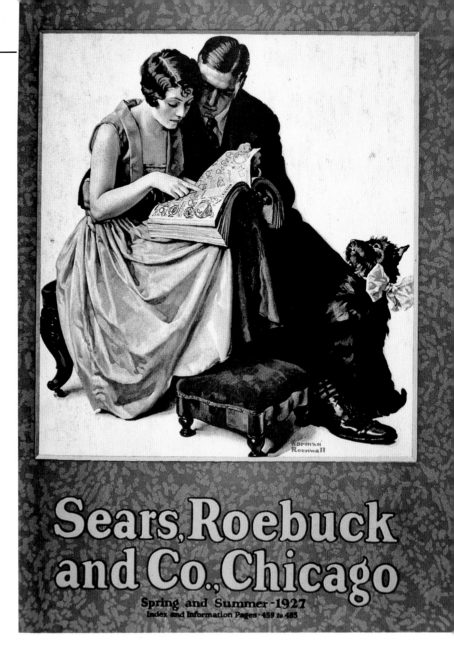

ABOVE: *The Sears Roebuck mail order catalog from 1927. Mail order tied rural America into the nation's increasingly urban-based economy, allowing anybody to purchase the most up-to-date goods.*

LEFT: *As more companies competed in similar markets, advertising became more important. Here, Uncle Sam promotes a cereal called Cream of Wheat in an advertisement from 1917.*

ABOVE: *A burned-out bus in London is evidence of the violence that accompanied the General Strike of 1926, when worker protests met with fierce government repression.*

lization of the franc. When price controls were lifted in 1918, the value of the franc fell from 20 cents to 6 and eventually to 2. In 1926 it was stabilized at one-fifth of its prewar value. The late 1920s saw a brief interlude of prosperity, ended by the Great Depression.

In the United Kingdom the cost of the war had been met by an annual budget that in 1918 was 13 times that of 1913; tax rates had risen fivefold, and the national debt, 14-fold. In the election that followed the Armistice the socialist Labour Party became the largest opposition party. An immediate postwar economic boom petered out by 1922.

In 1925 the government returned the pound to the gold standard, an international mechanism for valuing currencies against one another, in accordance with classical doctrine. At its prewar gold value, however, the pound was too expensive. Britain's exports, especially coal, were priced out of the world market. Export prices, notably wages, were cut in an attempt to make exports competitive.

In 1926 a general strike shut down industry and seemed to present a direct socialist challenge to the state itself. The government used troops to break the strike and passed legislation to weaken trade unions. At the same time, however, the government made some attempt to alleviate social hardship. The Widows', Orphans', and Old Age Contributory Pensions Act (1925) provided state support for underprivileged members of society.

The German question

The British economist John Maynard Keynes (1883–1946) was the most influential economist of the 20th century and one of the sternest opponents of the decision to return the pound to the gold standard. During World War I Keynes had worked for the government in the Treasury, which he officially represented at the Paris Peace Conference that formulated the treaties that ended the war (1919). Keynes opposed the economic terms of the Treaty of Versailles, particularly the harsh reparations it imposed on Germany and the constraints it placed on the German economy. Keynes resigned from his official position in order to write *The Economic Consequences of the Peace* (1919), in which he predicted the negative effect of German reparations on the European economy.

Germany, Keynes held, could not meet the amounts it owed out of any conceivable export earnings at a time when its industrial base was in chaos. The resulting dislocation of trade and finance would penalize not only the defeated country as it tried to rebuild its economy but all of Europe as well. At the geographical heart of the continent, one of its former strongest powers would be an economic wasteland. Resentment within Germany, meanwhile, led to political dissatisfaction.

Directly after the war this manifested itself in support for revolutionary communism; but as the 1920s went on, Germans began to seek consolation for unemployment and poverty from politicians of the far right. Adolf Hitler's Nazi party emerged from its origins in Bavaria in the mid–1920s and built national popular support. Hitler preached the restoration of national pride and aggressive German territorial expansion. The scapegoats Hitler blamed for Germany's plight were not the militarists who had led the country into World War I but socialists and, more ominously, Germany's Jews (*see* box, page 90).

LEFT: *An unemployed man in Detroit uses a placard to search for a job at the start of the Depression in 1930. While classical economics supported just such a self-reliant approach to unemployment, Keynes and his followers advised government intervention to supply jobs and thus maintain economic demand.*

The Great Depression

In 1929 a depression hit the world economy that was on a scale never before experienced. The so-called Great Depression, which lasted until 1934, caused economists to rethink their theories. In reacting to the depression, Keynes would formulate the most influential attack on neoclassical economics.

Since the Industrial Revolution the level of business activity in industrialized capitalist countries had veered from high to low, taking the economy with it. Economists defined such fluctuations as part of a regular business cycle. There was no general agreement on the causes of business fluctuations. Some economists

related them to episodes of speculation frequent in the 19th century, when easy borrowing encouraged periods of expansion. Contraction followed when banks called in their loans or when credit notes came due for redemption in hard money. Other economists believed that economic growth came in waves of growth of different length. Finally, poor times were associated with tightness in the money supply and the associated deflation of prices, as after the adoption of the gold standard in the United States in 1873.

The most able analyst of business cycles was U.S. economist Wesley Clair Mitchell (1874–1948), who made the subject his life work. An economist outside the classical tra-

Keynes and the New Deal

Keynesianism, the economic doctrine that dominated the period from 1945 to 1970, first became important in the late 1930s as a reaction to the Great Depression. The worldwide economic slump that began with the Wall Street Crash in October 1929 rapidly spread through Europe and the rest of the world, and left classical economists unable to explain either its length or its severity. By 1932 most banks in the United States were closed. Unemployment rose to 14 million in the United States, 6 million in Germany, and 3 million in Great Britain.

At the start of the depression economists disagreed about how much governments should interfere. Most maintained that it must be allowed to run its course as market forces eventually corrected the market. The conventional economic explanation for large-scale unemployment was in terms of rigidity in the labor market that prevented wages from falling to a level at which the market would be in equilibrium. The idea behind this sort of model of the labor market was that if there was large-scale unemployment, pressure from members of the labor force seeking work would bid down the wage to the point where, on the one hand, some of them would drop out of the labor market (that is, the supply of labor would fall), and on the other hand, firms would be willing to take on more labor because the lower wage would increase the profitability of hiring more labor. If, however, some rigidity prevented wages from falling to the equilibrium level at which the supply and demand for labor were brought into equality, unemployment would persist. Such an obstacle to the emergence of a market-clearing wage might be, for example, trade union action to maintain minimum wages or

ABOVE: President Franklin D. Roosevelt at his desk in the 1930s. Roosevelt's ability to communicate with ordinary Americans was important in restoring economic confidence.

minimum-wage legislation. The classical economists urged that the trade unions should be persuaded to accept a wage cut.

Other economists argued that government had a role to play not only in alleviating the social effects of the depression but also in kick-starting the ailing economy. According to the interpretation of the business cycle formulated by the British economist Arthur Pigou, for example, the optimism or pessimism of business leaders may influence an economic trend. During the early years of the Great Depression President Herbert Hoover appeared publicly optimistic about the inherent vigor of the American economy. Hoover's signals did not work, however, and failed to stimulate an economic upsurge.

The election of Franklin D. Roosevelt (1882–1945) in 1932 brought an administration to power committed to government intervention in the economy. The most important legislation of 1933 involved the major economic sectors, notably a new farm bill, the Agricultural Adjustment Act. It provided several mechanisms to help raise agricultural prices, but its most important feature was an agreement for farmers to reduce surplus crops in return for government payments. Support for agriculture has remained in place ever since. It remains a problem for classical economics that the support of agricultural prices is enforced in most industrial regions, such as Japan, the European Union, and the United States.

ABOVE: Famous U.S. economist J. K. Galbraith was one of Roosevelt's advisors and later also advised President John F. Kennedy.

The economic theory behind the New Deal was formulated by J. M. Keynes in his *General Theory of Employment, Interest, and Money* in 1936. Keynes challenged the bedrock of classical economics as expressed in Say's law, namely, that all income can be depended on to flow back in the form of demand for goods and services, and full employment. Keynes argued that the economy did not automatically tend to a state of full employment, and that market forces could not be relied on to pull it out of recession. Persistent unemployment might be caused by other factors than a disequilibrium in the labor market, such as, for example, a deficiency of demand for output. If businesses decided to cut their investment in new machinery at a time of full employment, for example, the machinery makers would lose their jobs and have less to spend on consumer goods, causing some of those who made consumer goods to lose their jobs as well. Thus a "multiplier" effect is set in motion, leaving the economy at a lower level of employment, incomes, and output than before.

Keynes argued that—in contrast to classical doctrine—there were no automatic forces at work in the economy to prevent such an occurrence. Wage cuts might reduce business costs, but they would also reduce what workers could buy, so that business could sell no more than before. Too little demand (that is, expenditure) in the economy would lead to high unemployment. Only government action to cut taxes or increase its own expenditure, even though that may mean a temporary budget deficit, could return the economy to full employment. The government had to ensure that demand in the economy was sufficient to create and maintain full employment, but not so great as to lead to inflation. In Keynes' theory, therefore, the public works schemes the Roosevelt administration launched to bring jobs to depressed areas such as the Tennessee Valley fulfilled precisely this purpose.

Keynes shared the classicists' view that savings and investment must be equal—where the money saved by people in savings organizations is then borrowed by firms to invest in capital equipment—but he maintained that they might not necessarily be equal only at full employment. Equilibrium can exist at different and even severe levels of unemployment. Low interest rates could not be counted on to increase investment, Keynes argued. Savers would not be attracted by only a nominal return that might not offset the advantages of holding liquid assets, and investment was not attractive in a market with excess capacity and no obviously favorable return. The answer, Keynes argued, lay in government intervention calculated to raise the level of investment spending. Only by running up a deliberate deficit in this way could the government break the underemployment equilibrium.

ABOVE: *Floodlights illuminate the Boulder Dam during its construction in 1935. The dam, now called the Hoover Dam, was built on the Colorado River as part of a New Deal plan to provide jobs.*

Keynes initiated a whole new area of economics that became known as macroeconomics. It concentrates on national economies and studying what determines national income, prices, and inflation, economic growth, the role of fiscal and monetary policy, and the determination of consumption and investment. Macroeconomics is distinguished from microeconomics, which covers the traditional area of economics: the market, supply and demand of individual goods and services, the pattern of their relative prices, the business firm, the entrepreneur, the problems of monopoly, competition, imperfect competition, and the theory of distribution. These topics continued to be mainly the preserve of neoclassical economists. Macroeconomics rests on microeconomic foundations, and the Keynesian "revolution" did not disrupt the neoclassical perception of the distribution of power among corporation, trade union, individual worker, and consumer.

In the words of the American economist J. K. Galbraith, "Keynes lifted the incubus of depression and unemployment off capitalism, or such was his design. He thus removed the feature that it could not explain, and which Marx had predicted would cause capitalism's downfall."

dition, Mitchell argued that every business cycle was unique because it emerged from a preceding set of events that were likewise unique. Mitchell identified and named four phases for a business cycle: prosperity, liquidation, depression, and recovery.

The Great Depression defied all economic understanding of the business cycle with its length and its severity. There was little sign of the recovery that most economists saw as the inevitable reaction to depression. In the United States President Franklin D. Roosevelt ignored economists who believed that governments should not interfere in the economy. Roosevelt's New Deal (*see* page 94) took steps to stimulate economic recovery while providing relief for the poorest members of society. The New Deal depended on Keynes' theories that business could be stimulated by providing jobs and pay that would be spent, thus stimulating the production of more goods.

The New Deal

The New Deal brought in higher taxes on the rich, strict regulations for private utilities, protection for the wage-bargaining process, and establishment of a set of fair employment standards. A huge relief appropriation of almost $5 billion reinvigorated several programs and funded a new federalized work relief program administered by the Works Progress Administration (WPA).

In 1935 Congress enacted the Social Security Act, which established a retirement fund, unemployment insurance, and local welfare grants. These programs, coupled with a subsidized public housing program, began what people called a welfare state (*see* box, page 100). By 1939, when the New Deal was over, the federal government not only had increased control over money supply and Federal Reserve policies (monetary policy) but also increased understanding of the economic consequences of its own taxing, borrowing, and spending (fiscal policy).

Orthodox economists in the United States generally accepted the New Deal, having no better suggestions, even though the measures introduced constraints on the market and allowed for the growth of the federal government, high taxation, and regulation of the economy. The business community, by contrast, saw welfare measures as a demotivating force for free enterprise. This attitude found expression in conservative administrations in the United States and Britain in the 1980s, but most welfare measures remain in place

Von Hayek and conservatism

The New Deal aroused opposition in some quarters and led to the emergence of conservatism as a distinct American political move-

ment. Conservatives urged a return to the free-market economy and retrenchment of the federal government and its bureaucracy. The movement found its clearest voice in *The Road to Serfdom* (1944) by the Austrian-born economist Friedrich A. von Hayek (*see* box) in which he argued that governments should not intervene in the control of inflation or other economic matters except by the restriction of the money supply.

Hayek and others subscribed to the over-investment theory of business cycles. They suggested that instability is the consequence of expanding production to the point where less efficient resources are drawn on. Production costs rise; and if they cannot be passed on to the consumer, the producer cuts back production and lays off workers.

ABOVE: A woman worker at the Army Arsenal in Philadelphia gauges cartridges during World War II. The conflict brought many U.S. women into the workforce for the first time.

Friedrich von Hayek

The Austrian-born British economist Friedrich von Hayek (1899–1992) was an influential conservative critic of Keynesianism and the the welfare state after World War II. After studying in Vienna and New York, he moved to London in 1931, where he held academic positions at the University of London and the London School of Economics. In his influential *The Road to Serfdom* (1944) Hayek argued that all government control of or intervention in a free market could only stall the threat of ills such as inflation or unemployment, not remove it. He suggested that the kind of piecemeal government interventions in the economy championed by Keynesianism would eventually lead only to domestic economic collapse. Those conditions, he believed, could only serve to pave the way for totalitarians to take power, much as Hitler had done in Germany in the 1920s and 1930s.

Drawing on a tradition of economic thought originating in the work of the Austrian Carl von Menger (1840–1921), von Hayek and his contemporary Ludwig von Mises (1880–1973) stressed the dynamic nature of markets. They considered the neo-classical model of price mechanism remote from the reality of market operation.

The Austrian school

Markets, according to the so-called Austrian school of economics, may tend toward equilibrium but are in reality in a constant state of disequilibrium. By assuming complete knowledge, meanwhile, neoclassical theory removed one of the most important functions of the market, which is the generation of the information that gives incentives for mutually advantageous exchanges to take place.

The Austrian school further argued that a socialist society, given the variety of human wants and the complexity of the capital and labor structure that needs to exist to satisfy them, is a theoretical and practical impossibility. Socialist welfare measures are thus a form of repression and the subsequent degradation of the human spirit. Monopoly was largely irrelevant and did not justify the greater evil of government intervention to prevent it. The focus was on the interlinkage between entrepreneurship and the competitive process as the key forces of coordination. For a well-ordered society the market must be complemented by appropriate political and social processes. The state's prime task in this society is to define and protect individuals' property rights and the means by which they are traded.

Gross National Product

In 1939 Adolf Hitler's growing aggression in Europe led to the outbreak of World War II. The United States joined the western Allies in December 1941, after the bombing of Pearl Harbor by the Japanese. Again, most of the world was involved in a traumatic conflict.

In the war's aftermath Keynesianism became the received wisdom in economics. The doctrine's concentration on demand as the key determinant of the level of output helped initiate a system of national income accounting. From Keynesianism emerged the study of the constituents of national output, or national income, with its related concept of gross national product (GNP). It is the measure of the final output of a country's economic activity. The size of a country's potential GNP depends on its factors of production—entrepreneurship, labor, capital, land and natural resources, and technology. Actual output will depend on the extent to which the labor force and the capital assets of a country are fully used. At any time output may fall below potential when either labor is unemployed or capital assets are not used to full capacity. Most nations today report Gross Domestic Product (GDP) rather than GNP. GDP is the value of all final goods and services produced in a country in a year.

Doing well through war

Keynesian statistical analysis confirmed what many Americans already knew: the war had been good for business. Stimulated by the need to provide for its own armies and those of its allies, the United States had almost doubled its Gross National Product between 1939 and 1944. Personal consumption had grown, and unemployment had fallen from 17.2 to 1.2 percent. Not even critics of Keynesianism could doubt that this remarkable economic growth was the result of public demand, demonstrated by an increase in federal government spending on goods and services from $22.8 billion to $269.7 billion. Keynesian doctrine became incorporated into U.S. law in the Employment Act of 1946. This act, which committed the government to maintaining high levels of employment and production to support high levels of demand, was a landmark. It represented the abandonment of laissez-faire as national policy. It also established the President's Council of Economic Advisers and required that the president submit an annual economic report to Congress.

In the United Kingdom, where Keynesian policies were put into effect in the 1940s, they continued until the late 1970s. The aim was to keep total demand growing in line with the economy's capacity to produce, so that it would be high enough to maintain full employment, but not so high as to generate inflation. It was only in the 1970s that some of the flaws of Keynesian theory became apparent.

Econometrics

In the 25 "good years" after World War II there was a revival of interest in econometrics, the mathematical formulation of economic relationships. Calculus, probability, statistics, linear programming, and game theory are used to analyze, interpret, and predict economic factors and systems, such as price and market action, production cost, and business trends. Econometric models are used as forecasting tools by corporations and governments.

Input-output analysis studies an economy in terms of the relationship between inputs and outputs. In the words of their inventor, Russian–American economist Wassily Leontief (see box), input-output analysis tables "describe the flow of goods and services between all the individual sectors of a national economy over a stated period of time." Leontief's method has had a major impact on economic thinking and has been widely used. Even such sophisticated models can deliver inaccurate forecasts, however. As U.S. economist J. K. Galbraith pointed out: "The equations linking change to result in [economic activity] are based on human judgments supported by statistical knowledge of such relationships in the past. Judgments can err; relationships can change."

The theory of the welfare state

One of the most significant responses to the Great Depression in the United States was the creation of the welfare state. The concept had

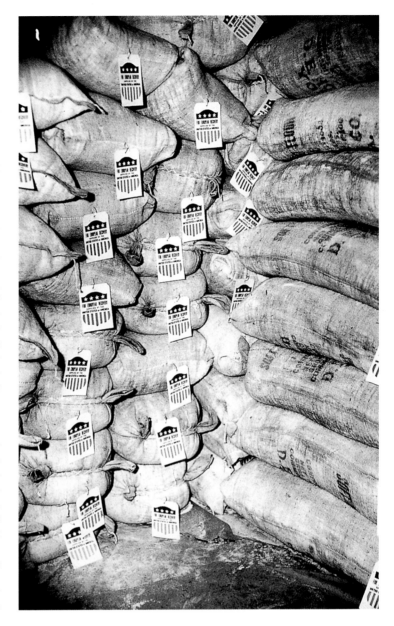

first emerged in the previous century in Germany, where, motivated mainly by fear of revolution, Chancellor Otto von Bismarck pushed through legislation from 1884 to 1887 relating to accident, sickness, old age, and disability insurance for most Germans. In Britain welfare legislation was passed in 1911 under the influence of the trade unions and middle-class socialist organizations such as the Fabian Society. It was not achieved without opposition. Britain was, after all, the birthplace of classical orthodoxy, which opposed government interference in the economy. In 1920, however, British economist Arthur C. Pigou (1877–1959) developed Alfred Marshall's ideas into a distinction between private and social costs, laying the basis of welfare theory as a branch of economic inquiry.

Classical economics did not support a redistribution of income. It held that the mar-

ABOVE: A shipment of flour supplied by the United States to Europe in 1948 as part of the Marshall Plan. The plan supplied $13 billion of aid to Western Europe to establish financial stability and expand trade, avoiding the economic problems experienced after World War I.

Wassily Leontief

Born in Saint Petersburg, Wassily Leontief (1906–1999) left Russia shortly after the Revolution and taught in Germany and at Harvard in the United States. Leontief studied the interdependence of the sectors of an economy. Economists have long understood that such an interdependence exists and have sought to codify its components. In Leontief's input–output theory the economy was an integrated system of flows or transfers from each activity of production, consumption, or distribution to each other activity. All these flows were set out in a rectangular table, the input–output matrix. The spread of output from one industry to the others could thus be identified, and adjustment in one part of the economy could be traced through to all the elements in the system. It was Leontief's achievement to tackle the problem by means of matrix algebra.

Modern computers have made input–output analysis a practical way of understanding economics. Interindustry tables were interesting for capitalism development and highly practical for socialist planning. Input–output analysis was applied in the Soviet Union, for example, in whose planned economy it was necessary to know what each industry required from another.

ginal utility of money differed from the marginal utility of goods. The marginal utility of money for the acquiring individual did not give any lessened satisfaction from the increments. Therefore, there was no economic case for transferring income or accumulated wealth from the rich to the poor. Pigou showed, however, that the marginal utility of money did indeed decline with increasing increment: in other words, the poor man or family got more enjoyment than the rich from an added increment in income. Pigou laid the economic foundation for a redistribution of wealth according to a social-welfare function that did not clash with orthodoxy.

As a result of the Great Depression and the example of the New Deal democratic governments began to intervene in the economy to correct the worst abuses of capitalism. The provision of a welfare state was promoted by the socialists and social democrats who since World War I had been the dominant force in the European labor movement.

Unlike the communists of the Soviet Union and elsewhere, who believed in the imposition of a planned economy, Europe's socialists largely accepted the basic rules of liberal democracy: free elections, civil rights, political pluralism, and the sovereignty of parliament. Between the wars socialists formed governments in numerous countries, typically in coalition with or supported by other parties. In Sweden, where social democrats have been politically more successful than elsewhere, they governed without interruption from 1932 to 1976.

Socialist reforms included the introduction of a comprehensive welfare system and the attainment of full employment using techniques of macroeconomic management developed by Keynes. In Great Britain welfare reforms were among the achievements of the first postwar Labour governments. Two important contributors to the emergence of British welfare economics were the Hungarians Nicholas Kaldor (1908–1986) and Eric Roll (b. 1907). Kaldor was a leading participant in the preparation of the Beveridge Report, which laid out the great postwar design for a cradle-to-grave welfare state. Eric Roll had a central role in the negotiations leading to the Marshall Plan and Britain's entry into the European Common Market.

Neocolonialism

In the decades following the end of World War II virtually all of Europe's former colonies won their independence, either peacefully or through war and bloodshed. Imperialism had

Government, welfare, and nationalization

The end of World War II left many of the warring nations devastated. Recovery, many people believed, could not be left to the market alone but should be shaped by government. There was a long precedent for such a belief. Since the 19th century there had been a gradual enlargement of government involvement in the economy, particularly in the provision of services such as education. In the late 19th century many countries passed public health acts and funded programs of planned urban growth. Pressure from reform groups had resulted in government action in the United States to break up business trusts and to enact health and safety measures to protect workers. The demands of the war economy in World War I had encouraged an even greater degree of government involvement in business. In the 1930s the New Deal of Franklin D. Roosevelt had set new levels of government involvement in business to stimulate a depressed economy and in the lives of citizens to protect them from the worst excesses of deprivation.

Government steps to aid recovery after World War II were thus another stage in a continuing process rather than wholly new. Many governments developed various welfare states, all of which took as their basis the idea that the self-reliance and private charity that had looked after the disadvantaged in the 19th century were no longer adequate. Government systems included the provision of free or subsidized health care, state pensions, disability and unemployment benefits, public housing, and other measures. Funding for such measures came from tax hikes or the imposition of national insurance payments on workers' earnings. State expenditure boomed. In 1929, for example, all government spending in the United States accounted for less than one-tenth of the country's GNP, or gross national product. Within 40 years government expenditure accounted for about one-third of the GNP, though more recently it has again become much smaller.

Welfare measures were unpopular with economists and politicians, who argued that they removed incentives to work, interfered with the market, or cost too much. Such critics were equally hostile to another manifestation of state intervention, nationalization, or taking vital industries from private hands into public ownership. Industries nationalized in various countries included energy production, transportation, and communications.

Some economists argued that the lack of competition and the lack of the need to make a profit would weaken nationalized industries. By the 1970s and 1980s their arguments seemed to have some truth, as nationalized industries throughout the West, by then a byword for inefficiency, were being returned to private hands in search of more competent management.

ABOVE: British mothers in London wait in line at a newly opened clinic of the National Health Service, which promised free health care for all. The mothers are bringing their babies for medical inspection.

long been condemned by its critics for its exploitation of native populations. The Soviet leader Lenin, for example, had declared that the great industrial powers owed their economic success to the imperial domains they had carved out in Africa, Asia, and the Pacific. The ruling powers and their workers lived on the backs of the deprived masses in the colonial lands.

Decolonization did not itself bring an end to such imperial exploitation, however. The new countries faced the problem of suddenly competing in the world economy outside the protective framework of the colonial system. Whatever its iniquities and morality, the system had served to encourage investment by the richer countries and provide ready markets for raw materials from the colonies.

Unable to compete on their own, in many cases the new states found themselves independent in name only. They were so tied to the economies of the Western nations that they remained subservient to the needs of the great corporations and multinationals of the developed world, which acted to monopolize their mineral resources and other commodities. Such a tied and unequal economic relationship was dubbed neocolonialism.

Critics of neocolonialism argued that it prolonged a situation in which markets favored industrialized countries. They continued to get raw materials cheaply from the undeveloped world, owned the technology that developing countries needed, and had the economic power to admit exports from the colonies only when it suited them. Developing countries could only grow, opponents of neocolonialism argued, if protected from the industrialized world and multinational investment. They argued that because markets would not themselves generate adequate growth and structural change, governments had to plan the new economies, using public-sector enterprises to provide the investments that the market would not.

Most Western economists, by contrast, considered that government interference in markets would be self-defeating because the markets played a positive role in economic development. Markets were impersonal and might not generate the kind of socially equable development many developing countries wanted, but they also attracted foreign investment that helped stimulate growth and the transfer of technology. Foreign economic aid would supply the additional savings and foreign exchange poor countries could not generate themselves.

Nonalignment and international debt

In the 1970s a movement grew up in the developing world called the Nonaligned Movement, demanding a correction of the inequities of the global economy. This move-

ABOVE: Teamsters strike Anchor Motor Freight in Wilmington, Delaware, in 1988. As monetarist theories resulted in tight control of the money supply, strikes became common as workers found themselves increasingly pressured into accepting lower wages or facing unemployment.

Milton Friedman

Milton Friedman (b. 1912) was one of the most influential and controversial economists of the late 20th century. After studying at various U.S. universities, Friedman joined the University of Chicago in 1946. Among his contributions to the development of classical economics, he became best known as one of the leading U.S. advocates of monetarism. The business cycle, the monetarist approach argues, is not determined by fiscal policy but by money supply and interest rates. By changing the amount of money in circulation and making credit either cheaper or more expensive, governments can avoid the boom-and-bust pattern typical of earlier capitalism. The Federal Reserve System is seen by many as crucial to maintaining price stability and economic growth.

Friedman believed that state provision of welfare undermined the values of individualism and self-help. In *Capitalism and Freedom* (1962), written with his wife Rose D. Friedman, he proposed scrapping welfare programs in favor of a negative income tax, which would guarantee an income. Friedman's ideas were highly influential during the 1980s, when monetarist policies were adopted by the governments of Ronald Reagan in the United States and Margaret Thatcher in Britain.

ment gained its greatest influence around the early 1970s, when the power of the oil-producing countries of the Middle East, who identified with the undeveloped world against the representatives of Western values, was at its height. Eventually, however, oil prices collapsed, and related swings in financial markets produced a problem of international indebtedness that weakened and divided the developing world. Following rising oil costs and deteriorating trade conditions for many raw materials in the later 1970s and 1980s, many developing nations had to pay more for their oil while receiving less for their exports.

The situation led to an increased dependence on large loans from commercial banks. Subsequent economic recession in the West resulted in even lower export earnings, however, and greatly increased interest rates on loans. At the end of the 1970s a new set of world leaders—Ronald Reagan in the United States, Margaret Thatcher in the United Kingdom, and Helmut Kohl in the Federal Republic of Germany—brought a new conservatism to international politics and economics.

In the 1980s, as a consequence, developing countries found it increasingly difficult to secure further loans from commercial banks and turned to an affiliate organization of the United Nations, the World Bank, for help. The latter began to provide loans only if recipient countries agreed to structural adjustment programs dictating that they had to adopt economic reform to reduce imports, promote "free-market" policies, and relax state controls. By 1990 nearly one-third of the World Bank's $22 billion budget was directed to encouraging such programs.

The shape of the World Bank

As the developing countries became independent, commercial banks, the International Monetary Fund (IMF), and the World Bank began to loan money for economic growth in these countries. These latter institutions were originally established, after a conference at Bretton Woods in the United States, to help Europe redevelop after World War II. Other multilateral development banks were later established for particular regions of the world in Asia, Africa, the Caribbean, and so on.

The World Bank is a family of institutions. It provides aid through two principal affiliates: the International Development Association (IDA) and the International Bank for Reconstruction and Development (IBRD). IDA aims to promote economic development through providing concessionary finance from funds contributed every three years by individual donor governments. By comparison,

LEFT: *Central banks, such as the Bank of England, became increasingly important in the 1980s as the chief means of regulating a country's money supply by changing interest rates.*

IBRD raises most of its funds on the world's financial markets and lends to developing countries at interest rates that tend to be somewhat below those of commercial banks and with longer maturities.

The Asian economies

Eastern and Southeast Asian economies tackled the problem of economic growth a different way. Despite the protective barriers erected by industrial countries, states such as Japan, Taiwan, Hong Kong, Singapore, and South Korea used technological innovation, cheap energy and labor costs, and product specialization to generate a rapid expansion of exports. Several circumstances contributed to their growth, including the lavish supply of U.S. aid after World War II and the rebuilding boom that followed.

In contrast to the economies of Asia, developing countries that practiced large-scale government intervention and trade protection were in difficulties by the end of the 1980s. With recession in the world economy they suffered unsustainable balance-of-payments and domestic deficits, rapid inflation, international debt, and very low growth. There began to emerge a worldwide consensus that a greater reliance on market forces was essential for speeding up development .

In the 1980s and early 1990s economies as different as China and India, Brazil and Tanzania were undergoing market-oriented reforms. The East and Southeast Asian experience for some was a triumph of the marketplace; for others it demonstrated the power of combining market forces with skillful government intervention.

The countries of East Asia, however, were not immune from economic collapse. They expanded production beyond market demand, leading in the mid-1990s to full-scale recession, with layoffs and factory closures in Japan. Korea, Malaysia, Thailand, Indonesia, and the other "tiger" economies faced the same danger of potential overproduction since a significant part of their growth lay in the same industries where Japan had overex-

Robert Lucas

Robert E. Lucas (b. 1937), an economist from the University of Chicago, has probably had more influence than anyone on recent research into macroeconomics. He investigated the theory of rational expectations, first devised by John Muth in 1961, which argued that economic agents such as individuals or firms, although they cannot completely know the future, will base economic decisions on information they can rationally expect to remain true.

The so-called Lucas critique argued that economists who promoted a change in policy must accept that the expectations of economic agents would also change. If workers believed that inflation would be 5 percent in a given year, for example, they might accept a 5 percent pay raise. If the government, however, expanded the money supply to allow 10 percent inflation, it might gain a short-term economic benefit, but people would come to expect higher inflation, and the policy would no longer work.

panded: car and other vehicle production, and electronics and computer hardware.

Monetarism

Inflation accompanied the full employment and rising standards of living enjoyed in most developed countries for the quarter of a century after World War II. Keynesians had recognized that if full employment was guaranteed by the government, a stable price level could not be maintained if trade unions could demand, and employers concede, whatever wage increases they liked. For this reason, governments implemented a series of incomes policies designed to reduce the size of wage and price increases. These policies had only limited success, however, and from the late 1960s there was a tendency for the inflation rate to accelerate alarmingly. Since the late 1970s Keynesianism has been largely displaced by monetarist arguments advocating low inflation over low unemployment.

Monetarism, the theory of macroeconomics particularly concerned with money supply, has a long tradition in the history of economic thought. As long ago as the 18th century economists such as David Hume put forward comparatively sophisticated explanations of the way in which an increase in the quantity of money would eventually affect prices. Contemporary monetarism, pioneered in the work of the American economist Milton Friedman (b. 1912) in the 1960s (see box, page 102), has its antecedents in the so-called "quantity theory of money," deriving from the work of the American mathematician and economist Irving Fisher (1867–1947).

In 1911 Fisher formulated an equation showing the price level as identically equal to the quantity of money multiplied by its "velocity of circulation"—the frequency with which a particular note or coin is spent—divided by the volume of transactions. Fisher held that prices would vary with the volume of money in circulation, with due allowance for its rate of turnover, or velocity, and the number of transactions involved. Upward movement of prices could be halted by reducing the money supply, downward movement by increasing the money supply.

Keynesians attacked this theory on the grounds that increases in the stock of money could lead to a fall in velocity of circulation and, in some circumstances, an increase in real income. Milton Friedman countered this objection by extending the Fisher equation to include other variables such as wealth and rates of interest, and developed a sophisticat-

BELOW: World leaders pose at the Bretton Woods hotel in New Hampshire in 1944. The conference established the World Bank as an organization for promoting economic development, first in war-torn Europe but later primarily in the nations of the developing world.

ed statistical method to evaluate it. Friedman maintained that the inflation that began to erode Keynesian economies in the 1960s and 1970s could be checked by strict control of the money supply. Using statistical techniques, he showed how this had happened in the past and therefore would in the future.

Demand for money

Friedmanite monetarists analyzed the individual's demand for money in the same terms as the demand for any other commodity: it was dependent on the individual's wealth and the relative price of the commodity in question. The basic idea of monetarist economics lies in the confrontation between the demand and supply of money balances. The authorities have power to determine the supply, since they control the amount of money created by the banking system. But people, not governments, decide how much in "real" money balances they wish to hold. If too much money is printed, people may try to get rid of the excess by buying goods or assets. If the economy is at full employment, this increase in expenditure will either raise the prices of home-produced goods or lead to a balance-of-payments deficit, causing the exchange rate to depreciate and pushing up import prices. In either case the rise in prices tends to reduce the "real" money balances that people hold.

Monetary policy involves controlling, via the central bank, the money supply and interest rates. They determine the availability and costs of loans to businesses. Tightening the money supply theoretically helps counter inflation; loosening the supply helps recovery from a recession. However, when inflation and recession occur simultaneously—a phenomenon often called stagflation—it is difficult for economists to know whether to tighten or loosen the money supply.

A central concept in inflationary theory since the mid-1950s has been the Phillips Curve, which relates the level of unemployment to the rate of inflation. The basic idea behind it is that lower unemployment leads to higher wage settlements, other things being equal. In the 1990s in the United States this has generally been the case, with low unemployment and relative price stability.

Critics of monetarism

James Tobin (b. 1918), winner of the Nobel Prize in Economics in 1981, criticized monetarism for its narrow interest on money. He pointed out that there is a whole range of financial assets that investors may be willing to hold in their portfolio, including not only money but also bonds and equities. Other economists, following the "rational expectations" theory developed by Robert Lucas, dispute whether a stable relationship exists between unemployment and the level of real wage demands, and hence whether there is such a thing as a "natural rate of unemployment" to begin with. They argue that the public will eventually recognize the link between the money supply and the price level, with the result that attempts to reduce unemployment by an expansion of the money supply will therefore have little lasting effect.

ABOVE: Workers assemble electronic circuit boards in a factory in Guangdong Province in the People's Republic of China. The globalization of the economy means that even formerly communist nations are increasingly part of the world's market-driven economy.

Today and tomorrow

During the second half of the 20th century the earth seemed to shrink because of improved communications and transportation, while global corporations grew until they became bigger than some of the world's countries.

Globalization has been defined by the Organization for Economic Cooperation and Development (OECD) as "the geographic dispersion of industrial and service activities and the cross-border networking of companies." Within the terms of this definition "service activities" are taken to include research and development, production, and distribution, while the term "cross-border networking" refers to joint ventures—business relationships set up to carry out a single project, such as marketing a new consumer product, and asset-sharing.

The globalization of economic activity has affected almost all aspects of contemporary life. It was the most important social phenomenon of the late 20th century and has touched governments, institutions, and individuals. Today all nations and every region, town, and village within them are parts of a world economy determined by global forces rather than by local ones. In essence, globalization is molding all the world's economic and technological forces into a single, shared social space.

How commerce took over the world

The growth of international trade since the end of World War II in 1945, and especially since the end of the Cold War in 1989, underlines the importance of globalization. Trade has reached unprecedented levels, both absolutely and in proportion to total world output. This process has been accelerated by improvements in transportation and communication, and by widespread deregulation—that is, the removal of old laws that restricted trade and controlled exchange rates.

During the second half of the 20th century new forces of competition transformed national economies to such an extent that today very few industries are based entirely on domestic markets alone. A firm in the construction industry, for example, may use local materials and labor, but it is more than likely to use imported capital equipment. It may even itself be a subsidiary of an international, foreign-based company. Global markets have emerged mainly as a result of the penetration of national markets, as many national and

ABOVE: The proliferation of advertisements in Moscow shows clearly how deeply and quickly Western capitalist values infiltrated Russia after the collapse of communism in 1991.

local firms have been forced to respond to worldwide demand and competition from firms based in other countries. Today, it is sometimes difficult to determine if a product has been foreign or domestically produced.

Although national differences still influence what each country produces, economic activity is now similar in most of the world's

Currency crashes

In the global marketplace, where currencies, firms, investment, and banking are bound by complex networks among numerous countries, even long-established economies can find themselves threatened. One example came in the United Kingdom in 1992, when the the U.K. currency, the pound sterling (£), came under intense pressure from currency speculators and threatened to plunge the economy into chaos.

The immediate cause of the crisis was Britain's membership in the Exchange Rate Mechanism (ERM), a system set up to maintain steady exchange rates among the currencies of the European Community (EC). When Britain joined in 1990, it committed itself to maintaining the value of the pound within a certain range of value against the German deutsche mark (DM). The Bank of England maintained the level of the pound by dealing in foreign currencies—if the value of the pound rose too high, it would sell its pounds to lower the value; if the pound fell too low, it would buy foreign currencies to raise its international value.

By September 1992 it had become apparent that the pound had been too highly valued against the DM. Investors, feeling they were not getting a good return, moved their funds elsewhere. The value of the pound plummeted. Speculators moved in on the money markets, repeatedly buying and selling vast quantities of pounds as the value rose or fell, making vast profits. In the face of aggressive speculation the Bank of England lost half its total reserves—about £12 billion—in a single day trying to prop up the value of the pound. It did not have strong enough reserves to withstand the pressure from speculators such as the financier George Soros, who personally made almost $1 billion on Black Wednesday. Britain was forced to leave the ERM, and the currency speculators moved on to look for another ailing currency.

Later in the 1990s currency speculation was at least partly responsible for stock-market crashes in Southeast Asia and Brazil. George Soros, meanwhile, has now largely repudiated the kind of dealing that made him billions of dollars. Increasingly involved in philanthropic organizations in the countries of the former Soviet bloc, Soros spends his time preaching against the kind of instability that currency dealing and a financial system based only on the confidence of investors brings to national currencies.

ABOVE: Chancellor of the Exchequer Norman Lamont announces Britain's withdrawal from the ERM in 1992.

Considering the financial crisis that shook Southeast Asia in 1997, Soros explained in his 1998 book *The Crisis of Global Capitalism* why he no longer believed in the market system: "The financial markets played a role that is very different from the one assigned to them by economic theory. Financial markets are supposed to swing like a pendulum. They may fluctuate wildly in response to shocks, but eventually they are supposed to come to rest at an equilibrium point. Instead, financial markets have behaved like a wrecking ball, swinging from country to country and knocking over the weaker ones."

nations. Even in countries where economic activity was previously tightly controlled, government regulation of business tends to be similar today. Businesses in New York, Budapest, and Shanghai operate fundamentally in the same way.

The world economy at the end of the 20th century could be split into three blocs related by their stage of economic development. The developed world includes the established economies of most of western Europe, the United States, and other advanced countries. The developing world describes India, many of the countries of the Pacific Rim and South America, some African states, and the former communist states of eastern Europe. In many such cases political change has left states which find that they have to participate in the global market in order to create economic growth. The undeveloped world, which includes the poorest nations, has little to trade in the international marketplace or lacks the infrastructure to do so.

Why go global?

Firms may seek to become global for a variety of reasons. Among the most compelling of them are the search for new markets and labor costs, since businesses naturally prefer to locate themselves in countries with the cheapest workforces. A local address may also enable what are basically foreign firms to avoid the tariff barriers that are traditionally used to restrict international trade.

Thus globalization has shifted the geographical location of economic activity to new

parts of the world. This has created challenges to the power of nation states within their own territories. As firms have grown and diversified internationally, increased global competitive pressures have forced governments to curtail state spending and intervention. One reason for this is that if governments attempt to tax powerful multinationals, the firms may take their business elsewhere.

Moving money

Globalization is sometimes seen as a limitation on governments' freedom to implement social policies such as health care and state pensions, two of the cornerstones of the welfare state. Although there is some truth in this view, it is nevertheless a generalization: the effect of the world economy is not the same in every country.

Finance is the most prominent and powerful force linking different parts of the world economy, and it has displayed the most spectacular symptoms of globalization in recent times. Financial reforms during the 1980s and 1990s, such as the lifting of exchange controls, have greatly facilitated the international movement of money. Currency speculators and investors, aided by advanced communications technology, are now able to move

enormous sums of money around the world at tremendous speed. The destructive power of this international financial system has been repeatedly demonstrated, notably in 1992, when speculation disrupted the European Union's Exchange Rate Mechanism (ERM) (*see* box, page 107), and in 1995, when international finance markets lost confidence in Mexico after three years of boom on the

ABOVE: The shoemaker Rebok was one of many multinationals which found that they could produce their goods much more cheaply in East Asia.
BELOW: Shell is one of many multinationals with wholly owned subsidiaries in many parts of the world.

Nick Leeson and the collapse of Barings Bank

The story of how Barings, one of the oldest banks in London, England, went bankrupt in 1995 as a direct result of the misguided market dealings of a single trader drew the world's attention to the precarious foundation of the international financial system. The collapse served as a timely reminder that financial markets are too mercurial to be accurately predicted or controled.

Nick Leeson, a young trader working for Barings' Singapore branch, was supposed to be "arbitraging"—that is, seeking to profit from differences between the prices of Nikkei-225 futures contracts listed on the Osaka Securities Exchange (OSE) in Japan and the Singapore Monetary Exchange (SIMEX). Such arbitrage involved buying "futures" contracts on one market and selling them on another. With small margins the volumes traded are usually large. However, the strategy is not usually very risky, since one position tends to offset the other.

Leeson's method of trading, however, went beyond normal methods of arbitrage. Instead of hedging his bets, he went for broke on the future direction of the Japanese markets. Between September and December 1994 his luck held, and he is thought to have earned his employers more than $150 million by the end of the year. These gains were achieved mainly through the clever use of "straddles" deals that make profits for the seller of the option provided that the markets prove to be less volatile than the option prices suggest.

Profits as large as this are never earned without a large measure of risk, as Leeson discovered when the Kobe earthquake struck on January 17, 1995. The scale of the disaster made foreign investors move vast sums out of Japan, and as a result, the Nikkei wobbled. In response to the falling Nikkei index Leeson bought futures on a huge scale in an attempt to push it back up. This would not have been easy for even the largest investor—the Tokyo stock market is the world's second largest—so naturally for Leeson alone it proved impossible. On January 23, 1995, the market plunged 1,000 points, and Leeson had no buying power left. More significantly, neither did his employer—Barings went bankrupt that very day.

Mexican stock exchange, causing the collapse of the peso.

The Mexican crash caused a "contagion effect"—a loss of confidence in similar emerging markets in other parts of the world. In 1997 poor growth forecasts for some East Asian countries led to a massive withdrawal of funds that caused their currencies to collapse. Such crashes underlined the extent to which short-term capital flows—both in to and out of a currency—can produce great instability throughout the system. Businesses whose interests were damaged by these crises were reluctant to leave their money in the affected countries or to make further investments of the same type. Pressures on an exchange rate are created partly by private speculators moving out of a currency but mainly by defecting institutional investors and multinational corporations.

New trading methods

Modern international finance has developed many new forms of international trade. Markets in "derivatives," for example, relate the price of the contract to the price of an underlying asset. The asset in question may be foreign exchange, bonds, equities, or commodities, and the volume of trading in derivatives could affect the prices of the underlying assets internationally. Derivatives enable investors to reduce the risk they bear due to market volatility but also permit them to undertake more risky deals in search of profit. There are also fears that they may increase the risks to the international financial system as a whole, as demonstrated in the

derivatives-related collapse of the London merchant bank Barings in 1995 (*see* box).

The other major consequence of the rise of globalization is the growth of multinational corporations. These huge corporate empires, which straddle the globe, have annual turnovers matching the GDP of many nations.

BELOW: *After the 1995 Kobe earthquake foreign investors feared that Japan's economy would slump as its resources were diverted from industry and poured into much-needed reconstruction.*

In 1998 there were 53,000 multinational corporations worldwide, with 450,000 subsidiaries that had global sales of $9.5 trillion. Together, the hundred largest corporations control 20 to 30 percent of global assets and employ six million workers worldwide. Multinationals have grown from national firms to global concerns using international investment to exploit their competitive advantages. Some multinationals are closely identified with one particular country, but their objective is always profit.

Many economists believe that global competition and production generated by multinationals increase the efficiency of the world economy. They say, for example, that multinational corporations encourage an international division of labor, so that countries become more specialized in producing goods in which they have a comparative advantage. Multinationals, they also argue, improve national domestic performance by introducing new technology and better working practices into the domestic economy; and by raising the skills of the national workforce, they act to everyone's benefit.

Clashes of interest

There may be conflicts of interest between multinational firms and individual nations, however, and there is evidence for a growing divergence between the priorities of the two. Revenue raised in one country by a multi-national may be used to finance investment in another. The multinationals' capacity to borrow from any nation according to the optimal exchange rate calls into question the effectiveness of any one nation's monetary policy. The fact that multinationals can transfer production from one country to another may undermine national industrial policy. It also enables corporations to put downward pressure on wages and working conditions.

Despite such facts, there is still evidence to suggest that pay and conditions for workers in multinationals compare reasonably well with domestic firms, at least in developing countries. More importantly for developed countries, multinationals transfer technology abroad with the result that in advanced countries skilled jobs are lost to low wage countries. Generally, the balance of power in multinationals has moved significantly from labor to capital, and the ability of corporations to organize production globally gives them enormous structural power relative to national governments and to labor.

The global markets

Globalization is welcomed by many economists as heralding a new era in which people everywhere are increasingly subjected to the rigorous disciplines of a worldwide marketplace. These changes have been driven by capitalism and technological growth, and have caused some traditional nation-states to

ABOVE: The headquarters of the European Economic Community (EEC) in Brussels, Belgium. The abandonment of tariffs within Europe has greatly facilitated the growth of multinational firms.

become little more than business units in a global economy. This view welcomes the emergence of global markets and the principle of global competition. The formation of transnational networks of production is bringing about a "denationalization" of economies. As national economies become drawn further into transnational and global flows, the authority and legitimacy of the nation state are increasingly challenged.

Reduced scope for protectionism

Nation-states have traditionally used trade protection to raise revenues, manage their balance of payments, and develop domestic industry. Globalization has left little scope for protectionism of this type. International institutions dedicated to the promotion of free trade, such as the World Trade Organization and the World Bank, have the power to enforce their decisions at national as well as international levels. The global regulation of trade by such bodies implies a significant reduction in traditional national sovereignty.

The decline of the welfare state

While classical and neoclassical economists generally welcome the triumph of individual autonomy and the market principle over state

power, left-wing commentators see it as an unwelcome victory for an oppressive global capitalism. Both schools of thought agree, however, that global capital imposes free-market economic discipline on all governments in the increasingly integrated global economy. Thus politics is no longer "the art of the possible" but rather the practice of "sound economic management." Governments now have to "manage" the social consequences of globalization in a context in which the constraints of competitive disciplines make social protection increasingly untenable and spell the demise of welfare-state policies.

According to neoclassical economists, global competition does not mean that no one can win without someone else losing—in economic terms, they are said to reject "zero-sum outcomes." Neoclassicalists and free marketeers argue that although particular groups within a country may be worse off as a result of global competition, almost all countries derive a comparative advantage from producing certain goods that can be exploited in the long run. Over time, the benefits of free trade and competition will "trickle down" to all members of society.

Other economists regard this view as over-optimistic, maintaining that global capitalism

BELOW: A redefining moment in history—the Brandenburg Gate in Berlin, Germany, as the wall that had divided the city was demolished in 1989.

creates and reinforces structural patterns of inequality within and between countries. Despite these differences of opinion, nearly all economists agree that traditional welfare options for social protection—such as care for the elderly, payments to those unable to work or unable to find a job—are now looking increasingly difficult to sustain.

Other economists believe that globalization conceals an actual increase in the power of at least some nation-states. According to them, the international economy is becoming increasingly regionalized into three major financial and trading blocs: Europe, Asia-Pacific, and North America. Far from developing toward a perfectly integrated world economy where the "law of one price" prevails, these skeptics claim, the evidence indicates only heightened levels of interaction among strong economies that remain predominantly nation-based.

Charges of neoimperialism

Another group believes that the intensification of worldwide trade and foreign investment is a new phase of Western imperialism in which national governments, as the agents of monopoly capital, are deeply implicated. Internationalization has been accompanied by the growing marginalization of many of the countries of the developing world, as trade and investment flows within the rich North intensify to the exclusion of much of the rest

of the globe. Some authorities take the view that "globalization" often reflects a politically convenient rationale for implementing unpopular orthodox neoclassical economic strategies.

GATT

The General Agreement on Tariffs and Trade (GATT) is an international organization that came into being as a forum for international tariff bargaining when 23 countries signed an agreement in 1947. Its Articles of Agreement pledged member states to expansion of multilateral trade with minimal barriers, the reduction of import tariffs and quotas, and the abolition of preferential trade agreements. By the time of the eighth set of negotiation meetings, which are known as the Uruguay Round (1986–1994), the membership of GATT included most of the countries in the world, and tariffs had been brought to an all-time low. The Uruguay Round concluded with an agreement that GATT should be superseded by the World Trade Organization (WTO), a more powerful institution with authority to make binding judgments where trade rules are disputed or broken.

Until the 1980s the industrialized countries' interest in openness of trade was not shared by many developing countries, which gave priority to building their own industrial base. Since the 1980s, however, developing countries have, on the whole, followed a different policy, rejecting protectionism and

LEFT: Logging is one of the chief targets for people arguing for sustainable development: a hillside cleared of rain forest to make new farmland in Malaysia.

ABOVE: El Niño—which is associated with climate change around the Pacific Rim and caused these landslides in Malibu, California—has been made worse by pollution caused by unrestrained economic activity such as the burning of fossil fuels.

reducing trade barriers. This new approach has been adopted partly because of changes in perception of the economic situation, and partly because of pressure from multilateral institutions such as the World Bank, the International Monetary Fund (IMF), and the WTO. Since the collapse of the Council for Mutual Economic Assistance (COMECON) in 1991 most of the former communist countries of eastern Europe have also liberalized their trade in line with Western countries. Thus there is now a truly global system of trade, with levels higher than ever before.

Not everyone agrees with the spread of free trade. The opening of a new round of WTO talks in Seattle in December 1999 was disrupted by the biggest mass protests seen in the United States since the Vietnam War, some of which broke into violent riots. The protesters, who ranged from environmentalists to church and labor groups and human rights campaigners, believed that the WTO's proposals to extend free trade would harm poorer nations. Lack of regulation, they argued, would leave such nations to be used only as sources of cheap material and labor by developed nations and global corporations.

Free-market economists believe that evolving global markets are created simply through deregulation. Other economists take an opposite viewpoint: that markets must be governed by common rules, and that the complexity of modern trade requires a detailed set of internationally obeyed laws and regulations for global market relations to function.

The modern reality

In the real world economic activity has synthesized both viewpoints. Extensive legal frameworks, such as the Single European Market and the North American Free Trade Area, have been drawn up for regional markets. The WTO works for greater trade liberalization but also concentrates on harmonizing domestic competition and business rules. This suggests that while economic activity will necessarily still be market-driven, a body of institutions is beginning to evolve to address the worst excesses of a completely unfettered economic system. In 1997, for example, members of the world's leading capitalist states—the G7, or Group of Seven—met in London, England, to discuss, specifically, how international coordination of national economic strategies might assist job growth across the G7 nations. This indicates a recognition of the fact that globalization needs to develop international institutions to tackle the macroeconomic problems of individual nations.

The search for sustainable growth

In the second half of the 20th century the effects of economic globalization on the environment became a subject of increasing political concern. Global warming, deforestation, increases in temperature, rises in sea levels, unpredictable meteorological activity—all these undesirable developments are connected with the global economic revolution but have no satisfactory solution in the doctrines of politicians. Although there has been an

LEFT: A mascot hands out leaflets during the 1992 Earth Summit in Rio de Janeiro, Brazil.

increase in public awareness of environmental problems in some countries, the risks of environmental globalization exceed by some way current capacities for addressing them.

The root cause of concern for most environmentalists is the apparent unsustainability of current trends in economic and social policy. Sustainable development is increasingly seen as a central concept. There are numerous definitions of the concept, which is difficult to describe accurately. In 1987 it was defined by the World Commission on Environment and Development (WCED) as "economic and social development that meets the needs of the current generation without undermining the ability of future generations to meet their own needs."

The rise of Green movements

From the late 1960s environmental campaigning organizations, such as Friends of the Earth, Greenpeace, and the World Wide Fund for Nature, have brought environmental or green issues to the attention of governments and the public. During the 1980s, however, a new phase of environmentalism began as people started to accept environmental protection as a matter for everyday concern. By

the mid-1990s a move to integrate environmental protection with social and economic policies led environmental activists to form partnerships, such as the collaboration between Greenpeace and the G-77 group of developing countries to influence the first review of the Convention on Climate Change agreed at the United Nations Earth Summit Conference at Rio de Janeiro in 1992.

The UN Conference on Environment and Development (UNCED), otherwise known as the Earth Summit, has now reached an important new set of agreements. They include a global plan for sustainable development, ranging from trade and environment, through agriculture and desertification, to capacity building and the transfer of technology. More specifically, UNCED has ratified various basic principles to integrate environmental and development policies. They include a new system of fines and incentives known as "the polluter pays"; a global consensus on the management, conservation, and sustainable development of the world's great forests; a legally binding agreement to stabilize greenhouse gases in the atmosphere; and legally binding agreements to conserve the world's species and to share fairly the diversity of the earth's ecosystem.

In the 1990s environmentalism entered a new phase. With governments in broad agreement over the gravity of environmental problems, sustainable development—defined by the United Nations' Environment Program (UNEP) as "development which improves people's quality of life, within the carrying capacity of the Earth's life-support system"—became a main objective for all parties. At the same time, pressure groups and coalitions of activists, working through specific and often emblematic issues, have sought to cause a fundamental shift in perceptions of the environment in the public at large.

The change in attitudes caused by these and other forms of activism quickly became apparent. In March 1995 Finland's Pekka Haavisto became the first member of a Green Party to join a national government, as minister for environment and planning. Two capital cities, Dublin (Ireland) and Rome (Italy), have had a Green mayor. Many of the democratic movements in eastern Europe had their roots in environmental groups. Beyond Europe a political group formerly known as

Values re-formed as the Green Party of New Zealand, while in Japan, the Seikatsu Club promotes "green" consumption and, with a turnover of some $300 million per year, has had a powerful say in the production of agricultural and manufactured goods.

By the close of the 20th century environmentalism had firmly established itself in the democratic process, with mainstream political parties having had to take "green" issues into their electoral agenda in order to remain attractive to their electorates. The environmentalists' political program urges policies involving minimum disruption of ecological processes, maximum conservation of materials and energy, and a static, rather than an increasing, population. Economic analysis of environmental issues involves tradeoffs. Identification of the opportunity costs involved can help policy makers reach the best decisions.

Moral issues

Globalization has had a significant impact on the sovereignty, autonomy, and politics of modern nation-states. As a result, it is now more difficult than ever before to regulate the

LEFT: There is increasing concern that industrial pollution is causing a growing hole in the ozone layer in the atmosphere over the Antarctic, showing as a dark patch in this space image from NASA.

BELOW: A leaking oil tanker off Luzon Island in the Philippines. Pollution like this is one of the worst negative externalities of human industry.

international arms industry. In an effort to overcome this new problem, a collective rather than a national approach has now been taken to questions of security, as evidenced by the global campaign to ban landmines and the establishment of an international court for crimes against humanity.

World military expenditure peaked at around $1 trillion in 1987. Although it has declined steadily since the end of the Cold War, the sheer quantity and destructive power of weapons are still high. Since the collapse of the Soviet Union the United States has dominated the arms' supply business; the other main arms' suppliers are the United Kingdom, France, China, Russia, and Germany, all of which have a vested interest in the sale of arms.

This transnationalization of the Western defense industrial base has been driven by commercial rather than domestic political factors. What is more, the same technologies that are revolutionizing various aspects of everyday life—from supermarket checkouts to personal computers and mobile phones—are transforming the logistics of war and the modern battlefield. As a result of these developments the traditional boundary between civil and military industrial sectors appears to be crumbling. Where there is no boundary, there would seem also less power to control events.

LEFT: The switch from leaded to unleaded gasoline was part of a concerted attempt to cause less damage to the environment.

BELOW: Helicopters for sale at the 1997 International Arms' Fair in Ankara, Turkey.

A new economic cycle

The end of the 20th century represented something of a crossroads for economists. The previous decades led some to be optimistic about the future. In 1987, for example, a stock-market crash in New York and London threatened to set off a global depression. To some economists and politicians the circumstances recalled those that launched the Great Depression of the 1930s. In fact, no such global economic collapse occurred, and the markets stabilized themselves.

Again in the 1990s currency and stock-market collapses in Southeast Asia, Russia, and Brazil threatened to upset the global economic balance. Commentators such as the financier-turned-philanthropist George Soros predicted that the role of the financial markets themselves was precipitating what Soros called, in the title of a book, *The Crisis of Global Capitalism*. For Soros it is a matter of time before the unrestricted markets create another Great Depression.

Other economists point to cause for optimism. The 1990s brought a certain amount of evidence that the political priority of industrialized nations for much of the century—how to achieve economic growth with low inflation—had been solved. Whether because of government policy or because of economic accident, inflation in many countries has dropped to only 2 or 3 percent a year. If this has come about as a result of fundamental economic change, then some people predict that the boom-and-bust cycle that has characterized capitalism might be growing weaker.

The shape of the future

There are signs, optimistically inclined economists argue, that the global economy is heading into a deflationary cycle in which costs will fall rather than rise. Computers, white goods, automobiles, some foods: the real prices of such goods has fallen steadily over the last decades. Partly this is a result of market competition, partly a result of globalization making available sources of cheaper materials and labor. Average pay settlements in industrialized countries have also had less inflationary pressure. In many countries the rising price of housing in an undersupplied market is the chief cause of inflation.

At the start of the new millennium the global economy was more truely global than ever. Some countries remained excluded from the wealth of the others, but virtually all were tied more closely in a network that made political or economic events in one nation of relevance to them all. How to harness the potential benefits of such a system and restrain its evils is the main challenge facing the new century.

ABOVE: Ethnic Albanian refugees returning to Kosovo in June 1999. Although the international community intervened in former Yugoslavia under the banner of the United Nations, the action was really a U.S. initiative in its role as the world's policeman.

SEE ALSO:

• Volume 4, page 35: International trade and finance

• Volume 4, page 63: The world economy

• Volume 4, page 93: International economic organizations

• Volume 5, page 25: Developing world

Glossary

accounts records of earnings, expenditure, assets, and liabilities kept by individuals, firms, and governments.

balance of payments a record of a country's international trade, borrowing, and lending.

balance of trade an indicator of a country's financial condition produced by subtracting the value of imports from the value of exports.

balance sheet a list of assets and liabilities that shows the financial condition of a firm, individual, or other economic unit.

barter a system of trading in which goods are exchanged for other goods rather than for money

black market an illegal part of the economy that is not subject to regulation or taxation and that often deals in high-priced, illegal or scarce commodities.

bond a legal obligation to pay a specified amount of money on a specified future date.

boom and bust a phrase that describes a period of wild swings in economic activity between growth and contraction.

business cycle the periodic but irregular fluctuation in economic activity, usually measured by GDP, which rises and falls for reasons economists do not fully understand.

capital the physical assets owned by a household, firm, or government, such as equipment, real estate, and machinery. Capital is also used to mean financial capital, or money used to finance a business venture.

capitalism an economic system based on private ownership and enterprise and the free market. Capitalism has been the dominant economic system in the western world since around the 16th century.

central bank a public organization, sometimes subject to government influence but often independent, established to oversee and regulate a country's monetary and financial institutions.

commodity a primary product such as coffee, cotton, copper, or rubber. In economics, "commodity" is also used to describe a good or service created by the process of production.

communism a political doctrine based on the ideas of the philosopher Karl Marx that seeks to establish social equality through central regulation of the economic activity and communal ownership. *See also* planned economies.

comparative advantage the advantage gained by a producer—an individual, firm, or government—if they can produce a good at a lower opportunity cost than any other producer.

consumer good an economic good or commodity that is bought for use by a household rather than by industry, for example.

consumer price index (CPI) an economic indicator based on the price of a range of goods and services to calculate an average for expenditure of a U.S. family.

cost benefit analysis the appraisal of a project or policy, for example, by comparing all the social and financial costs with the social and financial benefits arising from that project or policy.

curve a line plotted between points on a graph; an economic curve can be a straight line.

deflation a general downward movement of prices.

demand the desire for a particular good or service backed by the ability to pay for it.

depression a deep trough in the business cycle, usually marked by high prices and high unemployment.

developing country a poor country that is undergoing a process of economic modernization, typically including an increase of GDP through the development of an industrial and commercial base.

economies of scale factors which cause the average cost of producing a good to fall as output increases.

entrepreneurship the ability to perceive opportunities in the market and assemble factors of production to exploit those opportunities.

externality a cost or benefit falling on a third party as the result of an economic activity which is not accounted for by those carrying out that activity.

factors of production the productive resources of an economy, usually defined as land, labor, entrepreneurship, and capital.

fiscal policy the attempts a government makes to maintain economic balance by altering its spending on goods or services or its revenue-raising through taxation.

foreign exchange rate the rate at which one country's money is exchanged for another. The rate is often used as a measure of the relative strengths and weaknesses of different economies.

free trade international trade that is not subject to barriers such as tariffs or quotas.

gross domestic product (GDP) the total value of the final output within the borders of a particular economy.

gross national product (GNP) GDP plus the income accruing to domestic residents from investments abroad, less the income earned in the domestic market by foreigners abroad.

inflation an upward movement in the general level of prices.

interest the amount earned by savers or investors on their deposit or investment or paid by borrowers on their loan. The amount of interest is determined by the interest rate.

Keynesianism an economic doctrine based on the theories of J. M. Keynes that advocates government intervention through fiscal policy to stabilize fluctuations in the economy.

labor the workforce who provide muscle or brainpower for economic activity.

laissez-faire a French term for "let it do," originally used in classic economics to describe an economy with no government intervention.

land land and all natural resources such as oil, timber, and fish.

liquidity a measure of how easily an asset can be converted into cash.

macroeconomics the name given to the study of the economy as a whole rather than with the detailed choices of individuals or firms. *See also* microeconomics.

the market an arrangement which facilitates the buying and selling of a good, service, or factor of production. In a free market the prices which result from this are regulated by the laws of supply and demand rather than by external constraints.

mercantilism an economic policy popular in Europe from the 16th to the 18th centuries that stressed the importance of exports to earn reserves of gold and silver and used high tariffs to prevent imports.

microeconomics the study of individual households and firms, the choices they make in individual markets, and the effects of taxes and government regulation. *See also* macroeconomics.

monetarism an economic doctrine that regards the quantity of money in an economy as the main determinant of aggregate demand. As such, attempts by government to increase output by stimulating demand will only result in inflation.

monetary policy the attempt to regulate inflation and economic activity by varying the money supply and interest rates. Monetary policy is often the responsibility of a central bank.

money supply the amount of liquid assets in an economy that can easily be exchanged for goods and services, usually including notes, coins, and bank deposits that can be transferred by writing checks.

monopoly a market in which there is only one supplier of a good or service for which there is no close substitute.

neocolonialism a relationship between a country and a former colony in which the business interests of the first continue to dominate the economy of the latter.

opportunity cost the best alternative that must be given up when an economic choice is made.

planned economy an economy in which production and distribution are determined by a central authority, such as a ruler or a government.

private sector that part of an economy in which activity is decided and the means of production owned by individuals or firms rather than government. *See also* public sector.

productivity the ratio between the input of resources such as capital and labor and the resulting output of goods and services.

protectionism an economic doctrine that attempts to protect domestic producers by placing tariffs on imported goods.

public sector that part of an economy owned by a government or other public bodies such as state administrations.

recession a severe contraction of economic activity marked by two successive quarters of falling GDP.

specialization the decision by an individual, firm, or government to produce only one or a few goods or services.

sustainable development a form of economic growth that seeks to use renewable rather than finite resources and to minimize the permanent damage done to the environment by economic activity.

supply the quantity of a good or service available for sale at a particular price.

taxes and tariffs compulsory charges placed on economic activity by governments. Taxes might be placed on wealth or income, on business profits, as a sales tax on transactions, or as license fees on activities such as driving. Tariffs are taxes placed on imports into a country.

trusts anticompetitive alliances formed among businesses to force prices up and bring costs down. Trusts were outlawed in the United States by the Sherman Antitrust Act of 1890.

unemployment the condition of adult workers who do not have jobs and are looking for employment.

wealth the total assets of a household, firm, or country less its total liabilities.

welfare state a system of welfare provision by a government to keep its citizens healthy and free from poverty. Welfare provisions typically include free health care, insurance against sickness or unemployment, old age pensions, disability benefits, subsidized housing, and free education.

Further reading

Allen, L. *Encyclopedia of Money*. Santa Barbara, CA: ABC-Clio, 1999.

Ammer C., and Ammer, D. S. *Dictionary of Business and Economics*. New York: MacMillan Publishing Company, 1986.

Atrill, P. *Accounting and Finance for Non-Specialists*. Engelwood Cliffs, NJ: Prentice Hall, 1997.

Baker, J.C. *International Finance: Management, Markets, and Institutions*. Engelwood Cliffs, NJ: Prentice Hall, 1997.

Baites, B. *Europe and the Third World: From Colonisation to Decolonisation, 1500-1998*. New York: St. Martins Press, 1999.

Bannock, G., Davis, E., and Baxter, R.E. *The Economist Books Dictionary of Economics*. London: Profile Books, 1998.

Barilleaux, R.J. *American Government in Action: Principles, Process, Politics*. Englewood Cliffs, NJ: Prentice Hall, 1995.

Barr, N. *The Economics of the Welfare State*. Stanford, CA: Stanford University Press, 1999.

Barro, R.J. *Macroeconomics*. New York: John Wiley & Sons Inc, 1993.

Baumol, W.J., and Blinder, A.S. *Economics: Principles and Policy*. Forth Worth, TX: Dryden Press, 1998.

Begg, D., Fischer, S., and Dornbusch, R. *Economics*. London: McGraw-Hill, 1997.

Black, J.A. *Dictionary of Economics*. New York: Oxford University Press, 1997.

Blau, F.D., Ferber, M.A., and Winkler, A.E. *The Economics of Women, Men, and Work*. Engelwood Cliffs, NJ: Prentice Hall PTR, 1997.

Boyes, W. and Melvin, M. *Fundamentals of Economics*. Boston, MA: Houghton Mifflin Company, 1999.

Bradley, R.L., Jr. *Oil, Gas, and Government: The U.S. Experience*. Lanham, MD: Rowman and Littlefield, 1996.

Brewer, T.L., and Boyd, G. (ed.). *Globalizing America: the USA in World Integration*. Northampton, MA: Edward Elgar Publishing, 2000.

Brownlee, W.E. *Federal Taxation in America: A Short History*. New York: Cambridge University Press, 1996.

Buchholz, T.G. *From Here to Economy: A Short Cut to Economic Literacy*. New York: Plume, 1996.

Burkett, L., and Temple, T. *Money Matters for Teens Workbook: Age 15-18*. Moody Press, 1998.

Cameron, E. *Early Modern Europe: an Oxford History*. Oxford: Oxford University Press, 1999.

Chown, J.F. *A History of Money: from AD 800*. New York: Routledge, 1996.

Coleman, D. A. *Ecopolitics: Building a Green Society* by Daniel A. Coleman Piscataway, NJ: Rutgers University Press, 1994.

Cornes, R. *The Theory of Externalities, Public Goods, and Club Goods*. New York: Cambridge University Press, 1996.

Dalton, J. *How the Stock Market Works*. New York: Prentice Hall Press, 1993.

Daly, H.E. *Beyond Growth: the Economics of Sustainable Development*. Boston, MA: Beacon Press, 1997.

Dent, H.S., Jr. *The Roaring 2000s: Building the Wealth and Lifestyle you Desire in the Greatest Boom in History*. New York: Simon and Schuster, 1998.

Dicken, P. *Global Shift: Transforming the World Economy*. New York: The Guilford Press, 1998.

Economic Report of the President Transmitted to the Congress. Washington, D.C.: Government Publications Office, 1999.

Elliott, J. H. *The Old World and the New, 1492-1650*. Cambridge: Cambridge University Press, 1992.

Epping, R.C. *A Beginner's Guide to the World Economy*. New York: Vintage Books, 1995.

Ferrell, O.C., and Hirt, G. *Business: A Changing World*. Boston: McGraw Hill College Division, 1999.

Frankel, J.A. *Financial Markets and Monetary Policy*. Cambridge, MA: MIT Press, 1995.

Friedman, D.D. *Hidden Order: The Economics of Everyday Life*. New York: HarperCollins, 1997.

Friedman, M., and Friedman, R. *Free to Choose*. New York: Penguin, 1980.

Glink, I.R. *100 Questions You Should Ask About Your Personal Finances*. New York: Times Books, 1999.

Green, E. *Banking: an Illustrated History*. Oxford: Diane Publishing Co., 1999.

Greer, D.F. *Business, Government, and Society*. Engelwood Cliffs, NJ: Prentice Hall, 1993.

Griffin, R.W., and Ebert, R.J. *Business*. Engelwood Cliffs, NJ: Prentice Hall, 1998.

Hawken, P., et al. *Natural Capitalism: Creating the Next Industrial Revolution*. Boston, MA: Little Brown and Co., 1999.

Hegar, K.W., Pride, W.M., Hughes, R.J., and Kapoor, J. *Business*. Boston: Houghton Mifflin College, 1999.

Heilbroner, R. *The Worldly Philosophers*. New York: Penguin Books, 1991.

Heilbroner, R., and Thurow, L.C. *Economics Explained: Everything You Need to Know About How the Economy Works and Where It's Going*. Touchstone Books, 1998.

Hill, S.D. (ed.). *Consumer Sourcebook*. Detroit, MI: The Gale Group, 1999.

Hirsch, C., Summers, L., and Woods, S.D. *Taxation : Paying for Government*. Austin, TX: Steck-Vaughn Company, 1993.

Houthakker, H.S. *The Economics of Financial Markets*. New York: Oxford University Press, 1996.

Kaufman, H. *Interest Rates, the Markets, and the New Financial World*. New York: Times Books, 1986.

Keynes, J.M. *The General Theory of Employment, Interest, and Money*. New York: Harcourt, Brace, 1936.

Killingsworth, M.R. *Labor Supply*. New York: Cambridge University Press, 1983.

Kosters, M.H. (ed.). *The Effects of Minimum Wage on Employment*. Washington, D.C.: AEI Press, 1996.

Krugman, P.R., and Obstfeld, M. *International Economics: Theory and Policy*. Reading, MA: Addison-Wesley Publishing, 2000.

Landsburg, S.E. *The Armchair Economist: Economics and Everyday Life*. New York: Free Press (Simon and Schuster), 1995.

Lipsey, R.G., Ragan, C.T.S., and Courant, P.N. *Economics*. Reading, MA: Addison Wesley, 1997.

Levine, N. (ed.). *The U.S. and the EU: Economic Relations in a World of Transition*. Lanham, MD: University Press of America, 1996.

MacGregor Burns, J. (ed.). *Government by the People*. Engelwood Cliffs, NJ: Prentice Hall, 1997.

Magnusson, L. *Mercantilism*. New York: Routledge, 1995.

Mayer, T., Duesenberry, J.S., and Aliber, R.Z. *Money, Banking and the Economy*. New York: W.W. Norton and Company, 1996.

Mescon, M.H., Courtland, L.B., and Thill, J.V. *Business Today*. Engelwood Cliffs, NJ: Prentice Hall, 1998.

Morris, K.M, and Siegel, A.M. *The Wall Street Journal Guide to Understanding Personal Finance*. New York: Lightbulb Press Inc, 1997

Naylor, W. Patrick. *10 Steps to Financial Success: a Beginner's Guide to Saving and Investing*. New York: John Wiley & Sons, 1997.

Nelson, B.F., and Stubb, C.G. (ed.) *The European Union : Readings on the Theory and Practice of European Integration*. Boulder, CO: Lynne Rienner Publishers, 1998.

Nicholson, W. *Microeconomic Theory: Basic Principles and Extensions*. Forth Worth, TX: Dryden Press, 1998.

Nordlinger, E.A. *Isolationism Reconfigured: American Foreign Policy for a New Century*. Princeton, NJ: Princeton University Press, 1996.

Painter, D.S. *The Cold War*. New York: Routledge, 1999.

Parkin, M. *Economics.* Reading, MA: Addison-Wesley, 1990.

Parrillo, D.F. *The NASDAQ Handbook*. New York: Probus Publishing, 1992.

Porter, M.E. *On Competition.* Cambridge, MA: Harvard Business School Press, 1998.

Pounds, N.J.G. *An Economic History of Medieval Europe*. Reading, MA: Addison-Wesley, 1994.

Pugh, P., and Garrett, C. *Keynes for Beginners*. Cambridege, U.K.: Icon Books, 1993.

Rima, I.H. *Labor Markets in a Global Economy: An Introduction*. Armonk, NY: M.E. Sharpe, 1996.

Rius *Introducing Marx*. Cambridge, U.K.: Icon Books, 1999.

Rosenberg. J.M. *Dictionary of International Trade.* New York: John Wiley & Sons, 1993.

Rye, D.E. *1,001 Ways to Save, Grow, and Invest Your Money*. Franklin Lakes, NJ: Career Press Inc, 1999.

Rymes, T.K. *The Rise and Fall of Monetarism: The Re-emergence of a Keynesian Monetary Theory and Policy*. Northampton, MA: Edward Elgar Publishing, 1999.

Sachs, J.A., and Larrain, F.B. *Macroeconomics in the Global Economy*. Englewood Cliffs, NJ: Prentice Hall, 1993.

Shapiro, C., and Varian, H.R. *Information Rules: A Strategic Guide to the Network Economy*. Cambridge, MA: Harvard Business School, 1998.

Smith, A. *An Inquiry into the Nature and Causes of the Wealth of Nations*, Edwin Cannan (ed.). Chicago: University of Chicago Press, 1976.

Spulber, N. *The American Economy: the Struggle for Supremacy in the 21st Century*. New York: Cambridge University Press, 1995.

Stubbs, R., and Underhill, G. *Political Economy and the Changing Global Order*. New York: St. Martins Press, 1994.

Teece, D.J. *Economic Performance and the Theory of the Firm*. Northampton, MA: Edward Elgar Publishing, 1998.

Thurow, L.C. *The Future of Capitalism: How Today's Economic Forces Shape Tomorrow's World*. New York: Penguin, USA, 1997.

Tracy, J.A. *Accounting for Dummies*. Foster City, CA: IDG Books Worldwide, 1997.

Tufte, E. R. *Political Control of the Economy*. Princeton, NJ: Princeton University Press, 1978.

Varian, H.R. *Microeconomic Analysis*. New York: W.W. Norton and Company, 1992.

Veblen, T. *The Theory of the Leisure Class (Great Minds Series)*. Amherst, NY: Prometheus Books, 1998.

Wallis, J., and Dollery, B. *Market Failure, Government Failure, Leadership and Public Policy*. New York: St. Martin's Press, 1999.

Weaver, C.L. *The Crisis in Social Security: Economic and Political Origins*. Durham, NC: Duke University Press, 1992.

Werner, W., and Smith, S.T. *Wall Street*. New York: Columbia University Press, 1991.

Weygandt, J.J., and Kieso, D.E. (ed.). *Accounting Principles*. New York: John Wiley & Sons Inc, 1996.

Williams, J. (ed.). *Money. A History*. London: British Museum Press, 1997.

Websites

Consumer Product Safety Commission: http://www.cpsc.gov/

Equal Employment Opportunity Commission: http://www.eeoc.gov/

Environmental Protection Agency: http://www.epa.gov/

Federal Reserve System: http://www.federalreserve.gov/

Federal Trade Commission: http://www.ftc.gov/

Food and Drug Administration: http://www.fda.gov/

The Inland Revenue Service: http://www.irs.gov/

Occupational Health and Safety Administration: http://www.osha.gov/

Social Security Administration: http://www.ssa.gov/

The U.S. Chamber of Commerce: http://www.uschamber.com

The U.S. Labor Department: http://www.dol.gov/

The U.S. Treasury Department: http://www.treas.gov/

Picture Credits

Index

Fluvanna County High School
1918 Thomas Jefferson Parkway
Palmyra, VA 22963